# Life
*that*
## Matters

# A Life

## *that*

# Matters

*Inspiration and Encouragement
for Living with Purpose*

Kimberley Woodhouse

BARBOUR
PUBLISHING

Published by Barbour Publishing, Inc., P.O. Box 719, Uhrichsville, Ohio 44683, www.barbourbooks.com

*Our mission is to publish and distribute inspirational products offering exceptional value and biblical encouragement to the masses.*

Member of the
Evangelical Christian
Publishers Association

Printed in the United States of America.

# Introduction

Deep down, we have a longing. An intense desire to make our mark—to matter. We want to make every second count. But all too often, we're beaten down by life and hurdles that stand in our way. One after another, we stumble and fall.

My prayer as you read this book one entry at a time is simple:

Love Him. Seek Him. Live your life for Him. Throw off the shackles of guilt and discouragement. Bask in His grace, joy, and glory.

So that together, one day at a time, we can live lives that matter for Him.

Running toward the finish line,
Kimberley Woodhouse

# Run Your Race

Too many times we forget that each of us has been given our own unique race to run. Instead we get caught up in the competition around us. Our neighbor has a better-paying job. Our coworker has a brand-new car. Our friend leads three Bible Study classes a week, her house is immaculate, and her children are perfectly behaved.

In essence, we take our eyes off the finish line and focus on the runners in the lanes around us. We compare. We whine and grumble. We slow down or stop running altogether because we wonder why our race can't be as "good" as the next person's.

The analogy of our Christianity as a race should be a reminder to us daily. What do professional athletes do to achieve success? They train. Day in and day out. They focus on their own lane. They focus on the finish line. They don't stop and wave at the spectators. They don't stop to compare shoes with another runner.

> "The Bible uses many illustrations of athletes running a race in correlation with our Christian walk—so as believers, we should think of ourselves on par with Olympians. We don't stop. We don't start the race over. We run. Always keeping our eyes on the finish line."
>
> Unknown

They run. Focused totally on the race set before them.

As believers, it's important for us to train ourselves in scripture daily. We need to stay focused on the finish line—Jesus Christ.

Your race is your life, given to you by God—and it matters. Let's live in a way that glorifies Him.

## Scripture to Remember

> *Do you not know that those who run in a race*
> *all run, but only one receives the prize?*
> *Run in such a way that you may win.*
> 1 CORINTHIANS 9:24

> *Therefore, since we have so great a cloud of witnesses*
> *surrounding us, let us also lay aside every encumbrance and*
> *the sin which so easily entangles us, and let us run with*
> *endurance the race that is set before us, fixing our eyes on Jesus,*
> *the author and perfecter of faith, who for the joy set before*
> *Him endured the cross, despising the shame, and has sat down*
> *at the right hand of the throne of God.*
> HEBREWS 12:1–2

## Live It

* Don't compare yourself to others.
* Keep your eyes on the finish line.
* Stay focused, one step at a time.
* Let Jesus carry your burdens.
* Do your best.

# Be Kind

The Bible is very clear about being kind—but not just to those who are kind to us. We should be kind to those in leadership over us, those who work for us, and even those who despise us. We have the power to change society's perception of kindness just by the way we act in the grocery store line, in traffic, at work, and at home.

> "One who knows how to show and to accept kindness will be a friend better than any possession."
>
> SOPHOCLES

Our attitudes and actions are often a reflection of what our heart truly feels. Kindness begins in the heart, but we must choose to initiate it. So not only do we need to pray for guidance and a change of heart, but we also need to pray for the Lord to change our attitudes toward people. Especially those who have been unkind to us. Our sinful nature would advise us to treat others the same way they treat us, but Jesus instructs us differently. His perfect example of sacrifice for everyone—even those who persecuted and hated Him—demonstrates true kindness. As Christians, we should strive to be a living example of Christ everywhere we go.

## Scripture to Remember

*So, as those who have been chosen of God,*
*holy and beloved, put on a heart of compassion,*
*kindness, humility, gentleness and patience.*

COLOSSIANS 3:12

*"But love your enemies, and do good, and lend,*
*expecting nothing in return; and your reward will*
*be great, and you will be sons of the Most High;*
*for He Himself is kind to ungrateful and evil men."*

LUKE 6:35

*Be kind to one another, tender-hearted, forgiving*
*each other, just as God in Christ also has forgiven you.*

EPHESIANS 4:32

## Live It

* Smile at everyone you meet today.
* Offer a word of encouragement rather than criticism.
* Give a thank-you note to the cashier the next time you're in the line at the grocery store.
* Offer to help someone with a project around their home.
* Bring an extra cup of coffee to a neighbor or coworker.

# Be Positive

A positive outlook is always a better choice than a negative one. Even when the toughest things come our way, we can be positive about how we are growing through them and what lessons we are learning, always recognizing how amazing our God is.

Take this scenario, for example: Two drivers are involved in a fender bender at a stoplight. One driver yells and bangs his fist on the hood of his car—all the while complaining about how late he will be, how long the repairs will take, etc. The other driver is thankful that no one got hurt and recognizes the value in being grateful for the little things in life—to even be alive.

> "I am convinced that life is 10% what happens to me and 90% how I react to it."
>
> CHARLES SWINDOLL

If you were observing this scene, which driver would you want to ride with? The one ranting and raving? Or the one staying calm and positive in the midst of turmoil?

The answer should be an easy one. Thankfully we don't have to deal with these kinds of situations on a daily basis, but the choice to be positive *is* an everyday decision. Choose wisely and learn to embrace every day, no matter what obstacles stand in your way.

## Scripture to Remember

*But He said, "The things that are impossible*
*with people are possible with God."*
LUKE 18:27

*I can do all things through Him who strengthens me.*
PHILIPPIANS 4:13

*And God is able to make all grace abound to you,*
*so that always having all sufficiency in everything,*
*you may have an abundance for every good deed.*
2 CORINTHIANS 9:8

## Live It

* Make a promise to banish negative thinking as soon as it enters your mind.
* Seek positive ways to respond to those around you.
* Wake up each day and say, "Good morning, Lord!" rather than "Good Lord, it's morning."
* Start each day with a positive and uplifting scripture.
* Ask God to help change your negative thoughts into positive ones.

# Be Humble

In our competition to be the "best of the best," we often get caught up in attaining status, showing off our wealth, and climbing the social ladder. Humility and meekness fall by the wayside in favor of cutthroat strategies and flaunting the flashiest possessions. Many lust after the recognition of the spotlight, underestimating the satisfaction of self-sacrifice and anonymity. We are called to be humble, but how can we strike a healthy balance between our worldly pursuits and our biblical obligations?

The key is banishing pride. The Bible tells us that pride goes before the fall. It's because of our selfishness and pride that we covet things that aren't ours, bring others down so we can get ahead, and fail to put God first in our

> "Assuredly, Loving Souls, you should go to God with all humility and respect, humbling yourselves in His presence, especially when you remember your past ingratitude and sins."
>
> ALPHONSUS LIGUORI

lives. To be truly humble, we have to tackle our pride and rid ourselves of any arrogance. It's okay to strive for that big promotion, drive a nice car, and stand in the spotlight, but the end goal of our success should always be to serve others better. And remember to give God the credit whenever you can, because it's by His grace that we've been saved and showered with blessings— not our own doing.

## Scripture to Remember

*But He gives a greater grace. Therefore it says,*
*"GOD IS OPPOSED TO THE PROUD,*
*BUT GIVES GRACE TO THE HUMBLE."*
JAMES 4:6

*Do nothing from selfishness or empty conceit,*
*but with humility of mind regard one*
*another as more important than yourselves.*
PHILIPPIANS 2:3

*"For everyone who exalts himself will be humbled,*
*and he who humbles himself will be exalted."*
LUKE 14:11

*Be of the same mind toward one another; do not*
*be haughty in mind, but associate with the lowly.*
*Do not be wise in your own estimation.*
ROMANS 12:16

## Live It

* Go to the back of the line.
* Go to a soup kitchen and serve those less fortunate.
* Give God the glory when you are praised for your work.
* Volunteer to go on a mission trip to a third world country.
* Be a good sport.

# Be Enthusiastic

No one strives for mediocrity. Our primary goal in life isn't to just be *average*. So why do we often face each day with a ho-hum-just-another-day-at-the-grindstone attitude?

Being enthusiastic can change your outlook and help you encourage those around you. An enthusiastic person can help make insurmountable obstacles seem like attainable steps.

Paul's letter to the Colossians reminds us that everything we do should be glorifying to God, and we should praise Him in a thankful and enthusiastic manner.

> "I still get wildly enthusiastic about little things. . . . I play with leaves. I skip down the street and run against the wind."
> LEO BUSCAGLIA

Every moment we are given on this earth is a precious gift. Anyone who's lost a loved one understands this in a deep way. So no matter what you are facing today, whether a major corporate merger, flipping burgers, or cleaning toilets—remind yourself that even tying your shoes can be an act of worship. So put a smile on and face each day with enthusiasm.

## Scripture to Remember

*Whatever you do in word or deed, do all in the name of the Lord Jesus, giving thanks through Him to God the Father.*

COLOSSIANS 3:17

*Whatever you do, do your work heartily,
as for the Lord rather than for men.*

COLOSSIANS 3:23

## Live It

* Sing—give God the glory.
* Smile—even when it's tough.
* Choose to face everything with a positive attitude.
* Respond with positive and enthusiastic answers like, "Sure! I'd love to help."

# Study Your Bible

President Roosevelt's quote is a good one, but too many people today don't take it seriously. Many run blindly through their days and miss out on a deep and abiding relationship with the Lord that only comes from study of His Word.

The Bible is not just stories, history, and law. It's guidance, direction, comfort, answers, and truth. We know God better through the reading of scripture. We understand His precepts as we read the letters addressed to the New Testament churches. We can grasp the concept of grace and mercy by reading of His sacrifice and example.

> "A thorough knowledge of the Bible is worth more than a college education."
>
> THEODORE ROOSEVELT

The wealth of wisdom contained in scripture cannot be weighed or measured or compared. It is a lamp to our feet—the only true light to our often dark and narrow path.

Living for the Lord—a life that matters, this Christian life—means we need to make time every day to spend studying His word and learning more about our great God and Savior.

## Scripture to Remember

*Be diligent to present yourself approved to God
as a workman who does not need to be ashamed,
accurately handling the word of truth.*

2 TIMOTHY 2:15

*Your word I have treasured in my heart,
that I may not sin against You.*

PSALM 119:11

*Now these were more noble-minded than those in
Thessalonica, for they received the word with great
eagerness, examining the Scriptures daily to
see whether these things were so.*

ACTS 17:11

## Live It

* Resolve to read at least a few verses of the Bible every day.
* Start a new Bible study with a friend, and hold each other accountable.
* Aim to memorize one verse per week.
* Share your verse with at least one person.
* Have family devotions at least once per week.

# Be Willing to Sacrifice

A lot of people cringe at the thought of sacrifice. It means we have to give up something, and most of us don't like to do without. We're comfortable with our things and our stuff.

Jesus was very blunt with His followers about what it would take to follow Him, telling them that He had no place to even lay His head. Are you willing to sell all you own and follow Him if that is what He asks of you?

That's a really hard question, but sometimes the sacrifice asked of us isn't quite so radical. Are you willing to sacrifice your time to help with a project at church? What about sacrificing part of your income to support a child in another country? Or sacrificing your vacation to go on a mission trip?

> "I believe there is an obedience to the Gospel, there is a self-denial and a bearing of the cross, if you are to be a follower of Christ. Being a Christian is a serious business."
>
> BILLY GRAHAM

The amount or depth of our sacrifice isn't what's important. It's the willing heart behind the sacrifice. Jesus asks for us to be willing, to deny ourselves—to take up our cross and follow Him.

## Scripture to Remember

*But God demonstrates His own love toward us,*
*in that while we were yet sinners, Christ died for us.*
ROMANS 5:8

*Then Jesus said to His disciples, "If anyone*
*wishes to come after Me, he must deny himself,*
*and take up his cross and follow Me.*
MATTHEW 16:24

## Live It

* Think of one person whose agenda you can put first today. Offer to help him/her in any way you can.
* Give more than you receive.
* Offer to do a job that is unpleasant for someone else.
* Sacrifice your TV time to spend time with your kids.
* Sacrifice your coffee money to buy food for someone in need.

# Surrender Your Will

Most of us are willful and stubborn. We plan out our days, plan out the future—even plan for our kids' futures. But are we willing to surrender our plans, our *will*, over to the Lord?

The night before He died, Jesus went off to pray. He knew what was coming. He said, "Not My will, but Yours be done." As 100 percent man and 100 percent God, Jesus knew the sacrifice that He needed to make. For all

> "There are two kinds of people: those who say to God, 'Thy will be done,' and those to whom God says, 'All right, then, have it your way.'"
>
> C.S. Lewis

mankind. The weight of the world's sins—past, present, and future—was on His shoulders. He understood and accepted the pain and torment, torture and ridicule, that accompanied it. Yet He loved us enough to surrender His will to the Father so that we might have an eternity with Him.

Are you willing to surrender your will to Him? Because *His* will for your life is perfect. We may not understand now, or even in this lifetime, the purposes He has for us—but how wondrous it will be to hear, "Well done, my good and faithful servant."

## Scripture to Remember

*And He withdrew from them about a stone's throw,*
*and He knelt down and began to pray, saying,*
*"Father, if You are willing, remove this cup*
*from Me; yet not My will, but Yours be done."*
LUKE 22:41–42

## Live It

* Don't do anything today without first asking the Lord, "What would You have me do?"
* Ask the Lord to show you His will every hour.
* Let go of the urge to control things.
* Ask a friend to hold you accountable as you seek His will.

# Conquer Idleness

Idleness has become too easy in our technology-driven era. There's an app for this and an app for that. We have robot vacuum cleaners, voice-activated phones, and remote controls for everything. We can search the Internet 24-7 with our phones, iPads, and e-readers.

We've certainly benefited from technology, but it has also caused us to lead more sedentary lives. Kids don't play outside as much because there are video games, five hundred different channels on the TV, and the World Wide Web to occupy their time. Adults face many of the same temptations.

> "Determine never to be idle. No person will have occasion to complain of the want of time who never loses any. It is wonderful how much may be done if we are always doing."
>
> THOMAS JEFFERSON

More than ever, we need to be on guard about becoming idle. Rest, time with family, and play are all important aspects of our lives, but we need to watch out for idleness that leads to laziness. The enemy seeks to devour and destroy—distracting Christians from doing the Lord's work.

So stay alert. Set firm boundaries for TV and computer time. And don't allow idleness to take away from what matters most.

## Scripture to Remember

*Laziness casts into a deep sleep,*
*and an idle man will suffer hunger.*

PROVERBS 19:15

*She looks well to the ways of her household,*
*and does not eat the bread of idleness.*

PROVERBS 31:27

## Live It

 * Take a prayer walk. Ask God to help you in your quest to conquer idleness.
 * Set attainable goals.
 * Seek out volunteer work when you are tempted to be idle.
 * Exercise every day.

# Choose to Do What's Right

Peer pressure is difficult for children and teens to handle, but it can be even worse as an adult. Your coworkers, friends, church members, and even your family can put pressure on you to make decisions that *they* think are okay, but you know they are not the decisions God wants you to make.

It's one of the hardest things—standing alone on your island of conviction. But remember that you will never regret choosing to do what's right. You may regret feeling alone, abandoning friends and family, or hurting someone's feelings, but making a God-honoring choice will never leave you with a bad taste in your mouth.

First and foremost, always seek God's will. Pray about your decision. Don't be afraid to stand firm for what is right.

Peter—a man who loved Jesus with a passion most of us wish we had—even caved when the peer pressure became too much. He allowed fear to take over when he was asked if He was a follower of Christ. But Jesus loved Him and forgave Him, and Peter had the opportunity to later share his faith with thousands and choose what was right.

We can do the same.

> "It is the eternal struggle between these two principles—right and wrong—throughout the world. They are the two principles that have stood face-to-face from the beginning of time; and will ever continue to struggle."
>
> ABRAHAM LINCOLN

## Scripture to Remember

*Therefore, to one who knows the right thing
to do and does not do it, to him it is sin.*

JAMES 4:17

*Do not be overcome by evil,
but overcome evil with good.*

ROMANS 12:21

## Live It

✳ Examine your friends. Do they help you choose wisely?
✳ Think and pray before your speak or do anything.
✳ Take responsibility for your actions.
✳ Go to God's Word any time you are in doubt.

# Work on Your Harmony

*Harmony* is a pretty cool word. It pertains to music as well as relationships. And what better thing to associate personal harmony with than the sweetness of musical harmony?

Any simultaneous combination of tones can make musical harmony, but beautiful harmony that's pleasing to the ear only comes when just the right notes are played or sung together.

We can take an example from the old TV show, *I Love Lucy*. Lucy always wanted to be in Ricky's shows, but whenever she opened her mouth to sing along, she was off-key. Sometimes *way* off. And the sound that emanated

> "How can we live in harmony? First we need to know we are all madly in love with the same God."
>
> THOMAS AQUINAS

made everyone cringe. It's the same scenario we should strive to avoid in our Christian walk. We need to work toward being harmonious with other believers—not dissonant. Because the world is watching, and the strength of our testimony is dependent on our performance.

## Scripture to Remember

*So, as those who have been chosen of God, holy and beloved,*
*put on a heart of compassion, kindness, humility, gentleness*
*and patience; bearing with one another, and forgiving each*
*other, whoever has a complaint against anyone; just as the*
*Lord forgave you, so also should you. Beyond all these things*
*put on love, which is the perfect bond of unity.*

COLOSSIANS 3:12–14

## Live It

* Bite your tongue. Sometimes the best thing to say is nothing at all.
* Don't speak in anger or frustration.
* Give others respect. Listen, don't interrupt.
* Don't argue about petty things.
* Be courteous.

# Be a Good Friend

The old adage, to have a good friend, you must first be one, is true. But we have a tendency to be selfish and expect our friends to be there for us without being there for them in return.

The book of Romans tells us to be "devoted to one another in brotherly love" and to "give preference to one another in honor." *Devoted* is a powerful word. Are you devoted to your friends? Do you give them the attention they deserve?

Jesus commands us to love one another. But not just to love one another— to love one another as *He* has loved us. He loved us

> "There is nothing on this earth more to be prized than true friendship."
>
> THOMAS AQUINAS

so much He gave His life for us, took all the pain and shame and sin of the world upon Himself. Are we willing to do that for each other? That's the example He's given.

It's a tough challenge, but Jesus calls us to be good friends to one another. And it's a challenge we shouldn't take lightly. Spend some time today reflecting on how you can be a better friend—devoted and loyal. Love as He has loved us.

## Scripture to Remember

*"This is My commandment, that you love one another,
just as I have loved you. Greater love has no one
than this, that one lay down his life for his friends."*

JOHN 15:12–13

*Be devoted to one another in brotherly love;
give preference to one another in honor.*

ROMANS 12:10

*A friend loves at all times.*

PROVERBS 17:17

## Live It

* Offer an hour of time to a friend today.
* Pray for your friends.
* Write your friends encouraging notes, e-mails,
  texts—with an uplifting scripture.
* Don't try to fix your friends. Work on your
  own flaws and shortcomings.

# Be Joyful

Scripture is very clear that our life on earth will not be easy. Many times in the New Testament we see examples of Christians suffering. But through all this, we are also shown that we are to consider everything joy.

Being joyful doesn't mean that we must walk around with a permanent smile on our faces and that nothing will ever get us down. It also doesn't mean you have to fake an outer appearance of happiness

> "The ability to rejoice in any situation is a sign of spiritual maturity."
> BILLY GRAHAM

and joy. Why? Because joy comes from within.

We don't need lots of money to have joy. We don't need all our ducks in a row. We don't need everything to be running smoothly. We just need to be content in our circumstances, good or bad. Because we can trust that God is working in us and through us to bring us greater joy.

## Scripture to Remember

*Consider it all joy, my brethren,*
*when you encounter various trials.*
JAMES 1:2

*In this you greatly rejoice, even though now for a little while,*
*if necessary, you have been distressed by various trials.*
1 PETER 1:6

*And though you have not seen Him, you love Him, and*
*though you do not see Him now, but believe in Him, you*
*greatly rejoice with joy inexpressible and full of glory.*
1 PETER 1:8

*Rejoice in the Lord always; again I will say, rejoice!*
PHILIPPIANS 4:4

## Live It

* Make a list of your blessings.
* Look at all the stars tonight, and praise God for his handiwork.
* Perform random acts of kindness.
* Encourage someone else to find the joy in the midst of trials.
* Sing in the shower.

# Eat Right

Oh the temptations we face in this world. And the enemy loves to persuade us to give in. In America, one of our biggest problems is obesity. Too much food. Around almost every corner is another way to give in to gluttony. But we are bought with a price, and our bodies are a temple for the Holy Spirit. Shouldn't we be taking better care of ourselves?

> "The glutton digs his grave with his teeth."
>
> ENGLISH PROVERB

A perfect example of this is Jesus in the wilderness. For forty days and nights, He fasted. And then He allowed Satan to tempt Him. Can you imagine how weak he must have been after forty days? After one day without food, most of us would stuff just about anything in our mouths, but Jesus wouldn't. He resisted temptation and answered the devil with, "It is written, 'Man shall not live on bread alone, but on every word that proceeds out of the mouth of God'" (Matthew 4:4).

Next time we are tempted to indulge too much and be gluttonous, we need to remember this example. Let's turn to scripture instead of the snacks and remember that we are temples for Him. It's a high calling and one we need to honor.

## Scripture to Remember

*Or do you not know that your body is a temple of the Holy Spirit who is in you, whom you have from God, and that you are not your own? For you have been bought with a price: therefore glorify God in your body.*

1 Corinthians 6:19–20

*Whether, then, you eat or drink or whatever you do, do all to the glory of God.*

1 Corinthians 10:31

## Live It

* ✳ Commit each day to the Lord as soon as you wake up.
* ✳ Drink more water each day.
* ✳ Take vitamins.
* ✳ Try a new vegetable or fruit.

# Quit Bad Habits

Bad habits often start off small. But just like a snowball rolling down a hillside, they can grow rapidly. They can turn into drug addictions, alcoholism, gambling addictions, pornography, and adultery, etc. All have devastating consequences—destroying lives, marriages, and Christian testimonies.

Most studies say that it takes at least twenty-eight continuous days of a new, good habit to replace the bad habit. Are you willing to commit the next month to tackling one of your bad habits? The only way to do it is through constant prayer

> "Habit is habit, and not to be flung out of the window by any man, but coaxed downstairs a step at a time."
> MARK TWAIN

and commitment to the goal. Have an accountability partner that will pressure you to stay on track.

Practice memorizing scripture, and keep verses on index cards in your wallet or purse. Tape them to mirrors and desks to help remind you of your goal. Tackle that old self and put on the new one. As believers, we have been washed clean. Let's renew our minds and bodies by getting rid of one bad habit at a time.

## Scripture to Remember

*That, in reference to your former manner of life, you lay aside the old self, which is being corrupted in accordance with the lusts of deceit, and that you be renewed in the spirit of your mind, and put on the new self, which in the likeness of God has been created in righteousness and holiness of the truth.*

EPHESIANS 4:22–24

*Therefore I urge you, brethren, by the mercies of God, to present your bodies a living and holy sacrifice, acceptable to God, which is your spiritual service of worship. And do not be conformed to this world, but be transformed by the renewing of your mind, so that you may prove what the will of God is, that which is good and acceptable and perfect.*

ROMANS 12:1–2

## Live It

* Pray for God's guidance and help.
* Make a list of twelve habits you want to change, and tackle a new one each month.
* Fine yourself something of consequence every time you give in.
* Reward yourself when you have conquered a bad habit.

# Conquer Your Fears

Fear can destroy you. It is the root of worry and pride. The enemy loves to use fear to keep us from living our lives for the Lord.

The disciples learned this lesson the hard way after Jesus fed the five thousand. These men had spent so much time with their Lord and witnessed miracle after miracle, but still didn't get it. Jesus sent the crowds away, prayed, and then went to find his men on the sea. It was stormy. The men were frightened. And as Jesus approached them on the water, they thought He was a ghost.

> "The worst of all fears is the fear of living."
>
> THEODORE ROOSEVELT

They were gripped in fear. Fear of the storm, fear of the water, fear of the One walking on water. Only after he challenged Peter and calmed the storm did they worship Him and realize He was truly God's Son.

Fear is crippling. Don't let it get a foothold in your life. Don't be of "little faith." Instead, get out of the boat, and keep your eyes on the Savior. Because He will never leave you, and He can conquer every fear.

## A Life That Matters: Mary Slessor

Mary Slessor had many reasons to be afraid. Her father was an alcoholic throughout her childhood, and she was hesitant to act on her desire to serve the Lord out of embarrassment. She feared speaking in front of people and was at first intimidated by the warring tribes in Africa, where she began her mission work.

But stout, redheaded Mary followed God's call and used her sense of humor and strong faith to reach many Efik and Okoyong in Calabar. She is also recognized for being a driving force in the establishment of the Hope Waddell Training Institute.

## Scripture to Remember

*Even though I walk through the valley of the shadow*
*of death, I fear no evil, for You are with me;*
*Your rod and Your staff, they comfort me.*

PSALM 23:4

*"For I am the LORD your God, who upholds your right hand,*
*who says to you, 'Do not fear, I will help you.'"*

ISAIAH 41:13

*For God has not given us a spirit of timidity,*
*but of power and love and discipline.*

2 TIMOTHY 1:7

*So that we confidently say, "THE LORD IS*
*MY HELPER, I WILL NOT BE AFRAID.*
*WHAT WILL MAN DO TO ME?"*

HEBREWS 13:6

## Live It

* Remind yourself that God's strength is enough to conquer your fear.
* Face your fears as much as possible.
* Say Philippians 4:13 to yourself often.

# Serve Others

"Love your neighbor as yourself." Jesus heralded this commandment as one of the most important because he knew that our desire to live out all His other commands was linked to love. Just as the Good Samaritan stretched out his hand—and purse—across a barrier of hate, we should also reach out to one another in love.

Everyone has something to give. Don't be deceived into believing that you have nothing valuable to share. You don't have to start an international food bank or join the Peace Corps to serve others. It's easy if you start where you are—just serve the next person you see, and remember that small things do matter. You can make a difference one tiny service at a time. A seemingly insignificant act could mean the world to a person in need.

> "One can give without loving, but one cannot love without giving."
>
> AMY CARMICHAEL

It's easy to love people who return the sentiment, but it's often a struggle to love those who dislike you. Don't limit your aid to friends who appreciate your efforts. God also instructs us to love our enemies.

But simply doing good deeds isn't satisfying if your heart isn't in the right place—your actions must be based on love, or they will become just another burden you feel obligated to carry. Your attitude of servanthood must grow as an extension of your love for mankind. Then you'll begin to live a life of service that truly matters.

## A Life That Matters: Amy Carmichael

Despite her battle with neuralgia, a disease of the nerves that causes muscle pain and weakness, Amy Carmichael lived her life in service to the unwanted children of India. While traveling as a missionary throughout India in 1901, she uncovered the plight of countless young girls sold to the Hindu temples and forced into prostitution. This tragic discovery prompted Amy to found an orphanage called the Dohnavur Fellowship. She rescued hundreds of orphans from a life of poverty, neglect, and abuse and became known as *Amma,* or mother, to the children in her care. Today Dohnavur Fellowship is a 400-acre community with 500 residents, a hospital, and multiple children's nurseries.

## Scripture to Remember

*Each of you should use whatever gift you have received to serve others, as faithful stewards of God's grace in its various forms.*

1 Peter 4:10 niv

*For you have been called to live in freedom, my brothers and sisters. But don't use your freedom to satisfy your sinful nature. Instead, use your freedom to serve one another in love.*

Galatians 5:13 nlt

*Serve wholeheartedly, as if you were serving the Lord, not people.*

Ephesians 6:7 niv

*He who is greatest among you, let him be as the younger, and he who governs as he who serves. For who is greater, he who sits at the table, or he who serves? Is it not he who sits at the table? Yet I am among you as the One who serves.*

Luke 22:26–27 nkjv

*Rather, he [Jesus] made himself nothing by taking the very nature of a servant, being made in human likeness. . . . Therefore God exalted him to the highest place and gave him the name that is above every name.*

Philippians 2:7, 9 niv

## Live It

* Volunteer in your community.
* Hold open the door for someone.
* Buy lunch for a stranger.
* Mow your neighbor's lawn or shovel his driveway.
* Invite someone over for dinner.

# Get Organized

Some of us are born with the skill of organization and love to color-coordinate, file, and make Excel spreadsheets to help us manage our inventory, business, hours, and life in general. Others are not. Organizing is not easy, and it becomes simpler to let things slide, to be late (or miss!) appointments, to "fly by the seat of our pants."

Organizing may not come to you naturally and may even be a constant struggle, but the Bible clearly tells us that things should be done "properly and in an orderly manner." That doesn't mean you have to color-code everyone's sched-

> "Good order is the foundation of all things."
> EDMUND BURKE

ules on your calendar, but it does mean that we should work to keep things in order.

Just as God created everything in order—not chaos—we should follow His example. Organization saves time, stress, and worry. If it doesn't come naturally to you, it should be a priority to learn. It blesses your family and everyone around you.

## Scripture to Remember

*For God is not a God of confusion.*

*But all things must be done properly
and in an orderly manner.*

*In the beginning God created
the heavens and the earth.*

## Live It

* Find a place for everything, and always put it in its place.
* Donate things you haven't used in more than a year.
* Tackle daunting tasks by dedicating five to ten minutes to them each day.
* Mark a chart for yourself or your family to help you stay on top of things.

# Spend Time with Family

Scripture is clear that spending time with family is a key component in our lives. Each family member has a unique personality, and God gave you *your* family for a reason. Don't neglect one another, and don't get so caught up in the things of this world that you aren't taking the time to appreciate what God has given you.

It's our responsibility to encourage and support one another. A good Bible memorization program can bring your family together over scripture and give younger members a chance to help older ones. A time of worship and praise can encourage musical members of your family to share their gifts. No matter the activity, commit to sharing some quality, edifying time with your family.

> "As the family goes, so goes the nation and so goes the whole world in which we live."
>
> POPE JOHN PAUL II

## Scripture to Remember

*"These words, which I am commanding you today,
shall be on your heart. You shall teach them diligently
to your sons and shall talk of them when you sit in
your house and when you walk by the way and
when you lie down and when you rise up."*

DEUTERONOMY 6:6–7

*Train up a child in the way he should go:
and when he is old, he will not depart from it.*

PROVERBS 22:6 KJV

*Hear, O my son, and receive my sayings; and the years
of thy life shall be many. I have taught thee in the
way of wisdom; I have led thee in right paths.*

PROVERBS 4:10–11 KJV

## Live It

* Start or attend a family Bible study once a week.
* Schedule a family game night.
* Eat dinner together as much as possible.
* Ignore the phone when you are spending time together as a family.
* Pray for one another.

# Live with Integrity

As believers, integrity should be our way of life. We may be the only Jesus some will ever see, or the only Bible they will ever read.

It's becoming even more vital that society recognize what we have to offer. That we, as followers of Christ, have something that they need—a relationship with Him that leads to eternal life.

For the lost trying to fill a void in their lives by seeking worldly sources

> "Integrity means that if our private life was suddenly exposed, we'd have no reason to be ashamed or embarrassed. Integrity means our outward life is consistent with our inner convictions."
>
> BILLY GRAHAM

of happiness, we can be a quiet example of what really leads to a happy life. Are we being honest? Are we being trustworthy? What kind of TV shows are we watching? What language are we using? Are we living with integrity, and do our actions attract others to a Christ-centered life?

Integrity is much more than putting on a facade for other people. It's about being an example even when we know no one else is watching. It's doing what's right no matter what.

# A Life That Matters: Eric Liddell

A gold medal in the 400-meter dash at the 1924 Paris Olympics wasn't Eric Liddell's greatest accomplishment (although many people believe it was). Eric lived a life of integrity in every regard, and in the 1924 Olympics, he missed out on running his best event, the 100-meter dash, because the qualifying heat was on a Sunday, and Eric took the Sabbath very seriously. A missionary to China for more than two decades, Eric's legacy of integrity lives on, even being portrayed in the popular film *Chariots of Fire*.

## Scripture to Remember

*Finally, brethren, whatever is true, whatever is honorable,
whatever is right, whatever is pure, whatever is lovely,
whatever is of good repute, if there is any excellence and if
anything worthy of praise, dwell on these things.*

PHILIPPIANS 4:8

*"You shall have a full and just weight; you shall have
a full and just measure, that your days may be prolonged
in the land which the LORD your God gives you. For
everyone who does these things, everyone who acts unjustly
is an abomination to the LORD your God."*

DEUTERONOMY 25:15–16

*Do not lie to one another, since you laid aside the
old self with its evil practices, and have put on the new
self who is being renewed to a true knowledge according
to the image of the One who created him.*

COLOSSIANS 3:9–10

## Live It

✳ Be honest.
✳ Set high standards for yourself based on
  scripture.
✳ Dress modestly.
✳ Apologize to those you've offended or hurt.
✳ Be a servant to those around you.

# *G*et Involved in Your Church

Within the body of Christ, we all serve different vital roles. God has given each of us unique talents and abilities, and He wants us to use them in His church for His glory.

But a majority of churches have only a handful of volunteers, while the rest of the body simply fills the pews. But our call is to be active in our church. If all the parts of the body aren't present, how is it supposed to function?

Commit to becoming more active in your local church. What gifts and abilities can you apply that the Lord has given to you? Could you teach Sunday school? Lead a men's Bible study? Start a prayer lunch? Run the church library? Help in the nursery? All these things are

> "Christ's church is a place to grow people up in the Lord, not to enhance our leisure time."
>
> BILLY GRAHAM

essential members of the body so that it can learn and grow. Look past your pew. In what other capacity is God calling you to serve Him? Spend a week in prayer, and then approach your pastor about how you and your family can become more involved in the ministry of God's church.

## Scripture to Remember

*And let us consider how we may spur one another on toward*
*love and good deeds, not giving up meeting together,*
*as some are in the habit of doing, but encouraging one*
*another—and all the more as you see the Day approaching.*
HEBREWS 10:24–25 NIV

*For just as each of us has one body with many members,*
*and these members do not all have the same function,*
*so in Christ we, though many, form one body,*
*and each member belongs to all the others.*
ROMANS 12:4–5 NIV

*Now you are the body of Christ,*
*and each one of you is a part of it.*
1 CORINTHIANS 12:27 NIV

## Live It

* Join the choir or church band.
* Volunteer for children's church or the nursery.
* Volunteer to collect and circulate prayer requests.
* Teach a Bible study in your home.
* Volunteer to help clean or set up for special occasions.

# Take Responsibility
## of Your Finances

Sometimes our world seems to revolve around money. It takes money to buy food, clothes, a roof over our heads, clean water, electricity, transportation, insurance, and on and on and on. But too often, we pour so much of ourselves into making the money to pay the bills that we lose sight of what's really important. We get obsessed with money and it becomes our goal, or we slack in keeping good records of our finances stating that we don't want it to be our focus.

First and foremost, we need to remember that God will take care of us. That doesn't mean that we don't need to work, but it does mean that we need to stop worrying over money. Second, we need to remember that if we love money more than God, we've made it an idol. And what does money really give us? Are we taking any of this stuff with us? No. So let's get our perspective straight. Third, we need to be good stewards with what the Lord has given us. That means we need to be responsible with how we use our money, keep track of our money, and make sure that we are giving cheerfully.

> "God does not need our money. He owns everything, including 'our' money. What He wants [us] to discover is where our central focus of worship lies. Is that focus on God or our money?"
>
> BILLY GRAHAM

## Scripture to Remember

*And my God will supply all your needs*
*according to His riches in glory in Christ Jesus.*
PHILIPPIANS 4:19

*For the love of money is a root of all sorts of evil,*
*and some by longing for it have wandered away from*
*the faith and pierced themselves with many griefs.*
1 TIMOTHY 6:10

## Live It

* ✳ Tithe—give to God FIRST.
* ✳ Make a budget and stick to it.
* ✳ Give to others in need.
* ✳ Pray before every purchase.

# Exercise

We are challenged to glorify God with our bodies. We should not only focus on eating right and avoiding gluttony, but also on exercise.

The Bible doesn't say that we have to exercise so many times per day or so many times per week. It also doesn't provide Luke the physician's diet plan or outline the exact foods that Jesus ate every day. But it does give us the basics. We are to glorify God in our bodies, which means that if we aren't taking proper care of them, we can't go about the Lord's work.

> "Walking is the best possible exercise. Habituate yourself to walk very far."
>
> THOMAS JEFFERSON

So get out there and get your heart pumping. Praise God for the gift of life and another day to glorify Him through your body.

## Scripture to Remember

*But I discipline my body and make it my slave, so that, after I have preached to others, I myself will not be disqualified.*

1 CORINTHIANS 9:27

*Or do you not know that your body is a temple of the Holy Spirit who is in you, whom you have from God, and that you are not your own? For you have been bought with a price: therefore glorify God in your body.*

1 CORINTHIANS 6:19–20

## Live It

* Start a walking group at your church.
* Play with your children or grandchildren.
* Pray while you exercise.
* Schedule family outings that promote wellness.

# Make a New Friend and Keep Up with Old Ones

One of the great blessings of this life is friendships. But they don't always just land in our lap. Sometimes we need to reach out and make an effort to connect. And sometimes we tend to neglect and take for granted the friendships we've had for years, convincing ourselves that they'll still be there. They always have been, right?

These are obstacles worth tackling. Try to make an effort to reach out to someone new in your church,

> "The better part of one's life consists of his friendships."
>
> ABRAHAM LINCOLN

workplace, or neighborhood, and offer your friendship freely, expecting nothing in return. We never know how God will bless us through our relationships.

The Bible mentions a friend that sticks closer than a brother, and that there is no greater love than laying down your life for a friend. Remember that today as you make goals to better stay in touch with those who have made an impact on your life, those who have stuck through thick and thin. Praise God for the gift of friendship.

## Scripture to Remember

*A friend loves at all times.*

PROVERBS 17:17

*Two are better than one because they have a good return
for their labor. For if either of them falls, the one will
lift up his companion. But woe to the one who falls
when there is not another to lift him up.*

ECCLESIASTES 4:9–10

## Live It

* Send an e-mail, text, or letter to a friend.
* Make time to catch up and listen to your friends.
* Invite someone to a Bible study over coffee.

# Laugh

Watching a baby laugh is contagious, isn't it? Some of the most popular videos on YouTube showcase babies and small children laughing. Why? Because we long to laugh and feel the overwhelming joy that accompanies it.

In Proverbs, different translations say that laughter and a joyful heart are good medicine. Rather than getting bogged down with the stress, trials, temptations, and junk of everyday life, we should remind ourselves to laugh a little more often. It releases stress, and it makes us feel good.

> "The most wasted day is that in which we have not laughed."
>
> CHAMFORT

Laughter can go a long way in healing our physical and emotional hurts. Allow yourself the privilege of some good chuckles today, and laugh with abandon.

## Scripture to Remember

*A joyful heart is good medicine,*
*but a broken spirit dries up the bones.*
PROVERBS 17:22

*Then our mouth was filled with laughter and our tongue*
*with joyful shouting; then they said among the nations,*
*"The LORD has done great things for them."*
PSALM 126:2

*"He will yet fill your mouth with laughter*
*and your lips with shouting."*
JOB 8:21

## Live It

* Read a funny story.
* Make up a silly song in the car with your family.
* See who can come up with the funniest joke.
* Take silly pictures with your friends or family.
* Reminisce about past times that made you laugh.

# Accept Things You Can't Change

Life throws a lot of curveballs at us. Many things we can change, and likewise, there are many we cannot.

We tend to waste the most time on those things we can't change. Because we have a hard time accepting them. Because it's not part of our plan. Because we're not in control.

It's time to put our energy into the things that *can* change. The things the Lord would want us to be working toward—to be content in whatever circumstances we are in and move forward with His will for our lives.

> "God grant me the serenity to accept the things I cannot change, the courage to change the things I can, and the wisdom to know the difference."
>
> REINHOLD NIEBUHR

If we keep bucking the fences, they're still going to be there, and it's just going to wear us out. Why not put that energy into something that will move us forward rather than hold us back? Remember: through Him, we can do all things.

## Scripture to Remember

*Not that I speak from want, for I have learned to be content
in whatever circumstances I am. I know how to get along with
humble means, and I also know how to live in prosperity; in
any and every circumstance I have learned the secret of being
filled and going hungry, both of having abundance
and suffering need. I can do all things through
Him who strengthens me.*

PHILIPPIANS 4:11–13

*Therefore I am well content with weaknesses, with insults,
with distresses, with persecutions, with difficulties,
for Christ's sake; for when I am weak, then I am strong.*

2 CORINTHIANS 12:10

## Live It

* Don't dwell on things you have no control over.
* Let go. Let go. Let go.
* Memorize the serenity prayer and apply it to your life.
* Be creative at finding ways to find joy in the obstacles of life.

# Forgive

We are called to forgive others as we are forgiven by God. If we are unwilling to forgive, bitterness and hatred take root, and the consequences can be grave.

When asked by Peter, Jesus even said that we are to forgive four hundred and ninety times. That's a lot of forgiveness for just one person! But it ultimately amounts to very little when compared to the forgiveness of God. We continually mess up and wallow in sin, but He forgives us each and every time. How much more then should we forgive others around us?

> "Forgiveness is the final form of love."
>
> REINHOLD NIEBUHR

Through forgiveness we learn to love more fully—just as Christ loves us.

To forgive is not just to forgive someone who is sorry. We also must forgive those who aren't repentant. We never know what seeds can be planted by our example.

## A Life That Matters: Steve Saint

Steve Saint is the son of famous missionary pilot Nate Saint, who was killed along with Jim Elliot and three others by the Waodani Huaorani warriors they were trying to reach. Through the deaths of these men, the Waodani people did eventually hear the Gospel of Christ, in addition to many other peoples in Ecuador. Steve and his family returned to Ecuador to live among the people and became especially close to Mincaye, one of the tribesmen who killed his father. Forgiving the men who slayed his father opened the door for a precious friendship and testimony that has reached around the globe with books and movies touching millions of lives.

## Scripture to Remember

*Be kind to one another, tender-hearted, forgiving
each other, just as God in Christ also has forgiven you.*

EPHESIANS 4:32


*"Do not judge, and you will not be judged;
and do not condemn, and you will not be condemned;
pardon, and you will be pardoned."*

LUKE 6:37


*Bearing with one another, and forgiving each other,
whoever has a complaint against anyone;
just as the Lord forgave you, so also should you.*

COLOSSIANS 3:13


*Then Peter came and said to Him, "Lord, how often
shall my brother sin against me and I forgive him?
Up to seven times?" Jesus said to him, "I do not say to you,
up to seven times, but up to seventy times seven."*

MATTHEW 18:21–22


## Live It

* When you are tempted *not* to forgive,
  remember what Christ did for you.
* Remind yourself that no one is perfect.
* Forgive yourself—it will help you forgive
  others.
* Love one another.
* Forgive even when you don't want to.

# Simplify Your Life

An easy way to relieve stress, worry, physical ailments, scheduling issues, money problems, fights between the kids over toys, etc. is to simplify your life.

We live in a world filled with stuff. Our homes are filled with it. Our cars are filled with it. Our RVs are filled with it. Our garages are filled with it. Our sheds, our purses, our briefcases. . .all of it filled with stuff.

Think about small children at Christmas time. Parents are so excited for their little ones to open up the latest and greatest

> "Less is more."
> ROBERT BROWNING

toys they placed under the tree just for them. But once opened, children often wind up having more fun with the wrapping paper, bows, and boxes than with the actual toys.

Sometimes we just need to simplify and get back to the basics. Pick one area of your life at a time, and think through what could be simplified. Are you or the kids involved in too many activities? Do you spend too much money on stuff you don't need? Are you working too many hours to try to buy the stuff you don't need? Is everyone so scattered that you don't have time to spend together as a family?

Give this over to the Lord, and ask Him to guide you in the direction He wants you to go.

## Scripture to Remember

*"No servant can serve two masters; for either he will hate the one and love the other, or else he will be devoted to one and despise the other. You cannot serve God and wealth."*

LUKE 16:13

## Live It

* Budget your time wisely. Stay away from negative things.
* Don't allow your activities to rule your life.
* Limit things that take too much time away from God, your family, and your work.
* Get rid of unnecessary items that clutter your home or office.

# Set Goals

As we strive to improve our lives and make them more meaningful, we need to have goals to work toward. We won't achieve anything without a plan.

Think of your Christian life as a race with a prize at the end. To win the race, we have to keep working toward the goal. For example, to gain control of our finances, health, and spiritual well-being, we have to set goals to motivate ourselves and keep us focused.

Ultimately our lives should be lived for Christ. He is there at the finish line waiting for us, wanting to say, "Well done, my good and faithful servant."

Not many goals can be attained overnight. It is often a long and te-

> "The person who makes a success of living is the one who sees his goal steadily and aims for it unswervingly. That is dedication."
>
> CECIL B. DEMILLE

dious process. But setting smaller goals along the way to the larger ones reminds us to take everything one step at a time and to keep our eyes on the prize.

## Scripture to Remember

*Brethren, I do not regard myself as having laid hold of it yet;*
*but one thing I do: forgetting what lies behind and reaching*
*forward to what lies ahead, I press on toward the goal for the*
*prize of the upward call of God in Christ Jesus.*

PHILIPPIANS 3:13–14

*The plans of the diligent lead surely to advantage,*
*but everyone who is hasty comes surely to poverty.*

PROVERBS 21:5

*"For which one of you, when he wants to build a tower,*
*does not first sit down and calculate the cost*
*to see if he has enough to complete it?"*

LUKE 14:28

## Live It

* Make a list of goals you think the Lord would approve.
* Be realistic in the time frame of your goals.
* Set high standards, but avoid perfection.
* Persevere in your goals, even when you want to quit.
* Stay positive!

# Be Dependable

Can you imagine the world back in Noah's time? Evil reigned. It even says that the "wickedness of man was great on the earth, and that every intent of the thoughts of his heart was only evil continually" (Genesis 6:5). The Lord was grieved and sorry that He had put man on the earth. But Noah stood

> "Noah and his family were the only loyal and obedient subjects to the legal power: they alone were saved."
>
> ORSON PRATT

out. Noah found favor. Noah was dependable. Noah was trustworthy. He was chosen to carry on mankind when all else was to be wiped out.

What a job he was given! Over the span of a hundred years, he built an ark to God's specifications. Can you imagine the ridicule? The complaints? Yet Noah stood strong and dependable.

God is asking the same of us. He wants us to be dependable—even in the face of criticism and persecution. Dependable in our faith. Dependable in our relationships. Dependable in our work. This is honoring and pleasing to Him.

## Scripture to Remember

*In this case, moreover, it is required
of stewards that one be found trustworthy.*
1 CORINTHIANS 4:2

*But Noah found favor in the eyes of the LORD.*
GENESIS 6:8

## Live It

* ✳ Be there for your friends.
* ✳ Be on time.
* ✳ Don't overschedule yourself.
* ✳ Follow through with commitments.
* ✳ Avoid procrastination.

# Begin and End Your Day with Prayer

A life that matters is a life filled with prayer. Prayer is how we communicate with our Father through Jesus Christ. And those lines of communication need to continuously stay open.

If you are not in the habit of praying, a good way to begin is to start and end the day with prayer. I like to use the ACTS system: Start with

> "In the morning, prayer is the key that opens to us the treasures of God's mercies and blessings; in the evening, it is the key that shuts us up under His protection and safeguard."
>
> BILLY GRAHAM

*Adoration*, giving God the glory for all He's done in your life. Next is *Confession*. Confess your sins and give over all the guilt and doubt that accompanies them. Offer up *Thanksgiving*. Praise and thank God for all He has given you on a daily basis. Finally, *Supplication*. Even though God already knows what's in our hearts and on our minds, He wants His children to openly communicate with Him.

As you embrace the habit of praying every day, you will spend more and more time at the throne of grace adoring, confessing, thanking, and requesting.

## A Life That Matters: Billy Graham

From his humble beginnings as a dairy farmer in North Carolina to his rise as the man who's preached the Gospel to more live audiences than anyone else in history, Billy Graham is a man who has changed the world for Christ. His passion for the Lord and for evangelism is evident in the crusades and ministries he founded. When asked what the most important steps were in preparing for an evangelistic mission, he says, "My reply is always the same: prayer. . .prayer. . . prayer." Billy and Ruth Graham were both great prayer warriors. What an example to begin and end our days with prayer and live out a life on fire for Christ.

## Scripture to Remember

*"Keep watching and praying that you may not enter into temptation; the spirit is willing, but the flesh is weak."*
MATTHEW 26:41

*With all prayer and petition pray at all times in the Spirit, and with this in view, be on the alert with all perseverance and petition for all the saints.*
EPHESIANS 6:18

*Pray without ceasing.*
1 THESSALONIANS 5:17

*The end of all things is near. Therefore be alert and of sober mind so that you may pray.*
1 PETER 4:7 NIV

## Live It

* Start a prayer journal.
* Designate an area of your home as a "prayer corner."
* Ask your spouse to pray with you each morning and evening.
* Call a friend to pray with.

# Manage Your Time

To be good stewards of all God has given us, we must manage our time wisely. We shouldn't be lazy or idle, or likewise, racing around in chaos trying to keep up with everything.

> "Dost thou love life, then do not squander time, for that's the stuff life is made of."
>
> BENJAMIN FRANKLIN

Time management is one of the most sought-after skills. Whether you are a corporate CEO, a teacher, a janitor, or a homeschooling parent, what activities we dedicate our time to is important.

We need to be honoring God in the use of our time. Learn when to say no. Choose wisely which activities your family participates in. And most important, make sure you give the first portion of your time to God. When your time is managed well, there's a wonderful peace that comes with a job well done.

## Scripture to Remember

*Therefore be careful how you walk, not as unwise men but as wise, making the most of your time, because the days are evil.*

EPHESIANS 5:15–16

*The plans of the diligent lead surely to advantage, but everyone who is hasty comes surely to poverty.*

PROVERBS 21:5

## Live It

* Make a schedule for yourself and stick to it.
* Buy a planner to help you organize your time.
* Make a list of priorities.
* Measure twice, cut once.

# Put on the Fruit

We unknowingly touch so many people's lives every day. Why not make an effort to impact them in a wonderful and positive way? As Christians, we should be bearing much fruit. Galatians 5 gives us a beautiful list, but it's love that's the origin of everything.

The fruits of joy, peace, patience, kindness, goodness, faithfulness, gentleness, and self-control all come out of love. That's why Jesus said His greatest commandment was to love God and then to love your neighbor as yourself. Let's commit to putting on these fruits every morning and share God's love with the world.

> "The gracious, eternal God permits the spirit to green and bloom and to bring forth the most marvelous fruit, surpassing anything a tongue can express and a heart conceive."
>
> JOHANNES TAULER

## Scripture to Remember

*But the fruit of the Spirit is love, joy, peace, patience, kindness, goodness, faithfulness, gentleness, self-control; against such things there is no law.*

GALATIANS 5:22–23

## Live It

* Love the Lord your God.
* Love your neighbor.
* Love your coworkers.
* Love your enemies.
* Strive to set an example by your love.

# Find a Mentor, Be a Mentor

We are given many examples in scripture of mentorship, and we shouldn't ever get too old to have a mentor of our own. We should always be looking for the proverbial "Paul" in our lives. That spiritual mentor to help guide us and hold us accountable. And just like Paul in 1 Corinthians, our mentor should be an imitator of Christ.

> "The greatest influence in my life, other than the Bible, is my spiritual mentor."
>
> UNKNOWN

As we learn and grow in God's Word, we should then also be willing to mentor someone else. Sometimes we learn more by observing and by example. Other times, we learn more by teaching the same lesson ourselves.

God uses each stage of our Christian walk to bring us closer to Him. We must be willing to grow and to learn through each stage, whether it's following in the footsteps of a mentor, or becoming one ourselves.

## Scripture to Remember

*Be imitators of me, just as I also am of Christ.*
I CORINTHIANS 11:1

*Remember those who led you, who spoke the*
*word of God to you; and considering the*
*result of their conduct, imitate their faith.*
HEBREWS 13:7

## Live It

* Ask God to help you find a mentor in your church.
* Study the Word and grow.
* Become a mentor to someone spiritually younger than you.

# Stop Making Excuses

We're so good at making excuses. Nothing is ever our fault because we can blame it on someone or something else.

Instead we should be telling the truth to ourselves and others—owning up to our actions. This is key to living a life of honesty and integrity. Taking responsibility for our mistakes keeps us humble and continually willing to learn and grow.

When Jesus called people to follow Him, they either got up and followed or made excuses. Matthew, a tax collector, was one who got up and followed. Another said he would follow but wanted to bury his father first. Yet another said he would follow but wanted to say good-bye to his family first. Jesus listened to their excuses, but he wasn't asking them to follow Him when it was convenient. He was asking for them to follow Him *now*.

> "It is better to offer no excuse than a bad one."
> GEORGE WASHINGTON

We make the same kind of excuses. The pastor at church asks us to help with the mission board, but we insist we have no time to volunteer. We insist the money isn't there for a generous offering.

It's time to stop making excuses.

## Scripture to Remember

*"He who loves father or mother more than Me is not worthy of Me; and he who loves son or daughter more than Me is not worthy of Me. And he who does not take his cross and follow after Me is not worthy of Me. He who has found his life will lose it, and he who has lost his life for My sake will find it."*
MATTHEW 10:37–39

## Live It

* ❋ Don't make excuses.
* ❋ Own up to your mistakes.
* ❋ Don't make excuses.
* ❋ Be honest.
* ❋ Don't make excuses.

# Reach Out

When Christianity comes under attack, many believers pull back from sharing their faith. But it's not just in openly sharing the Gospel that we can touch lives for Christ. The slightest ray of light shone into someone else's life will often give that person pause to ponder, question, and seek out its source. Planting the seed is important, even if the first reaction to faith is aversion.

We are called to reach out—to meet people's needs right where they are—and consequently, show them the love of Jesus. Whether it's working a suicide hotline, sending a card to someone in the hospital, serving hot meals in a soup kitchen, or simply volunteering at a nursing home—

> "Too often we underestimate the power of a touch, a smile, a kind word, a listening ear, an honest compliment, or the smallest act of caring, all of which have the potential to turn a life around."
>
> LEO BUSCAGLIA

every act of kindness can help spread the Gospel in new and unique ways.

You may be the only way others see the love of our Father.

So get out in your community, and show people you care about them. Love them as Christ loves us.

## Scripture to Remember

*"A new commandment I give to you, that you love one another,*
*even as I have loved you, that you also love one another."*
JOHN 13:34

*"By this all men will know that you are*
*My disciples, if you have love for one another."*
JOHN 13:35

*And He said to them, "Go into all the world*
*and preach the gospel to all creation."*
MARK 16:15

## Live It

* Give everyone respect and love.
* Volunteer at a youth event.
* Encourage and express gratitude to those in the service industry.
* Bless the homeless by taking them useful gifts.

# Prioritize

"Get your priorities straight."

How many times have you heard that? From a family member? A boss? Your spouse?

We've all heard it a lot. But probably not enough. Because we often think of priorities as a simple agenda: what needs to be done first, second, third, and so on.

God has a different idea of prioritizing.

He wants to be first. Always.

Are you able to say that God and *His* agenda are at the forefront of your mind each and every moment of each and every day? None of us has attained that. . .yet. But that is what we should strive for.

If we maintain our focus on keeping Him first then the rest will fall into place. He will be guiding and directing us because our eyes will be on Him. We will be surrendered to His will. We will be loving Him and loving others.

> "There comes a moment when we all must realize that life is short and in the end the only thing that really counts is not how others see us, but how God sees us."
>
> BILLY GRAHAM

To prioritize God's way is simple: Keep Him first.

## Scripture to Remember

*"You shall have no other gods before Me."*

EXODUS 20:3

*"But seek first His kingdom and His righteousness,
and all these things will be added to you."*

MATTHEW 6:33

## Live It

* Adopt a new motto for yourself.
* Wake up and pray for God's will.
* Memorize Matthew 6:33 and Exodus 20:3.

# Always Do Your Best

It's so tempting sometimes to just do enough to get by. We're tired. We're stressed. We're overwhelmed. There's too much on our proverbial plate.

But we are bought with a price. Jesus gave His all on the cross for us. He gave up His life. Shouldn't we be willing to give Him everything as well?

Each task that is laid in front of us can be an act of worship. We are glorifying God in how we accomplish each task. Our goal shouldn't be mediocre praise. He's the God of the universe! He created *everything*. Billions upon billions of stars, planets, solar systems, and everything here on Earth. Our response to Him through our work and abilities and use of talent should be the very best we can give.

> "Your talent is God's gift to you. What you do with it is your gift back to God."
> LEO BUSCAGLIA

Praise Him through your gifts. Praise Him by doing your best. Praise Him with your talents. Praise Him by being a workman who does not need to be ashamed.

Do your very best.

## Scripture to Remember

*Be diligent to present yourself approved to God
as a workman who does not need to be ashamed,
accurately handling the word of truth.*

2 TIMOTHY 2:15

*Do you not know that those who run in a
race all run, but only one receives the prize?
Run in such a way that you may win.*

1 CORINTHIANS 9:24

*Whatever you do, do your work heartily, as for the
Lord rather than for men, knowing that from the
Lord you will receive the reward of the inheritance.
It is the Lord Christ whom you serve.*

COLOSSIANS 3:23–24

## Live It

* Always give 100 percent.
* Don't spread yourself too thin.
* Face your challenges like an Olympic athlete:
  never compromise.
* Focus on one thing at a time.
* Don't dwell on past mistakes.

# Watch Less TV

Television is a tough habit to break, but we need to get rid of the things in our lives that are not glorifying to God. While TV can be used for good and educational purposes, most of the time it isn't.

In 2010, the average American watched 2.7 hours of TV a day. That amounts to over 40 days worth of TV a year. And that's the most conservative statistic out there. Nielsen's blog states that Americans are watching more TV than ever—an average of 153 hours per month, which would add up to over 1,800 hours a year.

> "Our minds are molded in many different ways—often in ways we are not aware of at the time. I am convinced that many things—the films we watch, the television we see, the music we listen to, the books we read—have great effect on us."
>
> BILLY GRAHAM

We could all probably afford to cut out some of our TV time. Instead, you could lead a Bible study, take a walk with your spouse, or volunteer to help with your child's Little League team. The possibilities are endless.

Examine how much time you spend glued to the tube, and start giving some up for God.

## Scripture to Remember

*Making the most of your time, because the*
*days are evil. So then do not be foolish,*
*but understand what the will of the Lord is.*

EPHESIANS 5:16–17

*How long will you lie down, O sluggard? When will*
*you arise from your sleep? "A little sleep, a little slumber,*
*a little folding of the hands to rest"—your poverty will*
*come in like a vagabond and your need like an armed man.*

PROVERBS 6:9–11

## Live It

* Play a game with your family.
* Turn off the TV at dinner.
* Teach your kids how to cook.
* Start a Bible study with your family.

# Persevere

There's a story told about the great pianist, Ignace Paderewski, and a little boy playing "Chopsticks" together on stage. The story goes that the little boy was taken to the pianist's concert by his mother. Before the concert, the boy was drawn to the shiny black piano and took to the stage to start playing "Chopsticks." The crowd reacted in anger, but Paderewski appeared behind

> "When you reach the end of your rope, tie a knot in it and hang on."
> THOMAS JEFFERSON

the boy, playing a counter-melody and encouraging the child, "Keep going. Don't quit, son. Keep playing. Don't quit."

The story may or may not be true, but it's a beautiful illustration that reminds us no matter what level of ability we have, we should resist the urge to quit because the Master is there beside us reminding us to persevere.

We all face pretty tough scenarios in our lives, but we never truly face the end of our rope because our great Savior is waiting there with open arms to carry us through.

## Scripture to Remember

*Pay close attention to yourself and to your teaching;*
*persevere in these things, for as you do this you will ensure*
*salvation both for yourself and for those who hear you.*

1 TIMOTHY 4:16

*Blessed is a man who perseveres under trial; for once*
*he has been approved, he will receive the crown of life*
*which the Lord has promised to those who love Him.*

JAMES 1:12

## Live It

* Even when you're tired, don't quit.
* Keep going.
* Don't quit.
* Seek strength from God.
* Memorize James 1:2–4. (The NIV translation uses the word *perseverance*.)

# Practice Patience

Most of us have probably seen the little cartoon of the monk on the hilltop speaking softly to God, "Lord, grant me patience. . ." Then the monk raises his voice to continue, "And I want it right now!"

In this age of instant everything, we have grown accustomed to getting what we want, and *fast*. Phones put us in touch with almost anyone at the touch of a button. And Skype lets us communicate with people around the world and "in person" via a camera and computer screen.

Patience is one of those lovely characteristics that we have to practice. It doesn't always come easy. It doesn't always come when we want it. But we are instructed to practice it nonetheless. We are to wait on the Lord. Be

> "Patience and diligence, like faith, remove mountains."
> WILLIAM PENN

patient and understanding with each other, always showing love.

So. . .let's practice patience. Ready, set. . .go!

## Scripture to Remember

*Therefore I, the prisoner of the Lord, implore you to walk
in a manner worthy of the calling with which you have
been called, with all humility and gentleness, with patience,
showing tolerance for one another in love, being diligent to
preserve the unity of the Spirit in the bond of peace.*

EPHESIANS 4:1–3

*Rest in the LORD and wait patiently for Him;
do not fret because of him who prospers in his way,
because of the man who carries out wicked schemes.
Cease from anger and forsake wrath; do not fret; it leads
only to evildoing. For evildoers will be cut off, but those
who wait for the LORD, they will inherit the land.*

PSALM 37:7–9

*Love is patient, love is kind and is not jealous;
love does not brag and is not arrogant.*

1 CORINTHIANS 13:4

## Live It

* Make a list of other people who've had to wait for you.
* Let someone go ahead of you in line this week.
* Count to ten before you do anything.
* Pray for patience.

# Balance Work and Play

Some people are workaholics while others are "playaholics." But according to scripture, there is a time for everything, and we need to seek balance in all things. The only way to find balance is to seek the Lord's will and strive to honor Him in everything. Easier said than done. But a heart focused on Him, sincerely yearning to please Him, will not miss the mark.

> "Our schedules are so hectic we can't get everything done, or else we are bored and restless, constantly looking for something to amuse us. We are the most frantic generation in history—and also the most entertained. The Bible tells us that both extremes are wrong."
>
> BILLY GRAHAM

The Lord doesn't intend for us to work our fingers to the bone and have no time for refreshment. Neither does He want us to while away our time with frivolous activities that have no eternal value. The key is in seeking His will for our lives and always looking to Him for the balance we need.

Seek wise counsel, read the Word, and pray for His guidance.

## Scripture to Remember

*Be of sober spirit, be on the alert. Your adversary, the devil,*
*prowls around like a roaring lion, seeking someone to devour.*
1 PETER 5:8

*It is not good to eat much honey,*
*nor is it glory to search out one's own glory.*
PROVERBS 25:27

## Live It

* Take time to work and play every day.
* Demonstrate your goal of balance by sharing your schedule with your kids.
* Plan a work day for your family and a play day for your family.

# Be Honest

It's so simple, and yet it's one of the biggest struggles we face. Honesty.

Some people say white lies, or half-truths, are okay, but that's just an excuse. We tell lies partially out of fear. We're afraid of getting in trouble and what others might think of us. But fear is not of the Lord, remember?

> "Honesty is the first chapter in the book of wisdom."
>
> THOMAS JEFFERSON

Let's start tackling this beast of honesty. Scripture tells us that a lying tongue is an abomination to the Lord. But when we are honest with ourselves and with one another, it truly can change our lives. We can set an example for others and pass down honesty to future generations, one truth at a time.

## A Life That Matters: Abraham Lincoln

Our sixteenth president was given the nickname Honest Abe long before he took on the role of president. In speeches, conversations, and business dealings—he was known for always telling the absolute truth. There are many sources that cite Abraham Lincoln thrived on honesty even as a store clerk. One story describes him accidentally short-changing a customer and after realizing the error, Mr. Lincoln tracked down the customer to return the full amount with an apology. He's also credited with walking several miles to correct a mismeasurement on his part.

Abraham Lincoln, known as one of the favorite presidents of our country, certainly earned his nickname of Honest Abe. Isn't that the kind of person we want in leadership?

## Scripture to Remember

*O Lord, who may abide in Your tent? Who may dwell on Your holy hill? He who walks with integrity, and works righteousness, and speaks truth in his heart. He does not slander with his tongue, nor does evil to his neighbor, nor takes up a reproach against his friend.*

PSALM 15:1–3

## Live It

* Tell the truth.
* Pray for guidance in *all* your dealings.
* Always ask, WWJD? (What would Jesus do?)

# Perfect Practice

The old saying "Practice makes perfect" isn't true. Especially in the case of piano practice, if you continually practice the same thing incorrectly, you will never make it perfect. But going back and correcting your mistakes and practicing again *will* make it perfect over time. With much practice.

So what does this teach us? We continue to fail and fall into sin. But the closer we get to the Lord on our spiritual walk, the more we see the imperfections that need to be worked on. Working on one thing at a time and fixing the problems helps us to *practice*—live our lives in a way that is pleasing to Him.

> "Practice does not make perfect. Only perfect practice makes perfect."
>
> Vince Lombardi

So let's change our mind-set. Only *perfect* practice will make it perfect. Let's keep our eyes on Jesus, who is perfect, and work on the blemishes in our lives one at a time.

## Scripture to Remember

*"But he who practices the truth comes to the Light, so that his deeds may be manifested as having been wrought in God."*

JOHN 3:21

*For he who lacks these qualities is blind or short-sighted, having forgotten his purification from his former sins. Therefore, brethren, be all the more diligent to make certain about His calling and choosing you; for as long as you practice these things, you will never stumble; for in this way the entrance into the eternal kingdom of our Lord and Savior Jesus Christ will be abundantly supplied to you.*

2 PETER 1:9–11

## Live It

* Learn from constructive criticism.
* Don't be a know-it-all.
* Strive to do every job the right way the first time.
* Always take your time.

# Learn to Say No

Saying no is so hard to do. Especially when it is something we really want to do. Or something we think we should do. Or something that we think will help somebody.

But one of the best things we can do for ourselves and for our family is to learn to say no to the things that aren't the very best use of our time. In seeking the Lord's presence and His will for our lives, we need to be seeking what *He* wants us to do. What His *best* is.

By saying yes to every opportunity offered to us, that's one more opportunity

> "Good, better, best.
> Never let it rest.
> Till your good is better
> and your better best."
>
> SAINT JEROME

we're depriving someone else of. If we overextend ourselves, we'll inadvertently turn enjoyable tasks into stressful ones. That's why it's essential to follow the "Good, Better, Best" code and only say yes to the things which are the very best.

## Scripture to Remember

*Now as they were traveling along, He entered a village; and a woman named Martha welcomed Him into her home. She had a sister called Mary, who was seated at the Lord's feet, listening to His word. But Martha was distracted with all her preparations; and she came up to Him and said, "Lord, do You not care that my sister has left me to do all the serving alone? Then tell her to help me." But the Lord answered and said to her, "Martha, Martha, you are worried and bothered about so many things; but only one thing is necessary, for Mary has chosen the good part, which shall not be taken away from her."*

LUKE 10:38–42

## Live It

* Pray before each decision.
* Don't overbook yourself.
* Work on saying no in a kind and loving manner.

# Encourage Others

Life can be difficult. Some of the things we deal with in this world are downright devastating and overwhelming. But every disaster is an opportunity to rise up as a source of encouragement.

Sometimes encouragement comes in the form of a hug; sometimes it's in walking alongside a person who's struggling or hurting. Sometimes encouragement is needed to prod someone to do what's right.

> "Correction does much, but encouragement does more."
>
> Johann Wolfgang von Goethe

In our world of negativity, we can shine a positive light by encouraging those around us. The Lord will present you with opportunity after opportunity to serve Him by encouraging others around you. After all, encouragement comes from the Greek word *parakaleo*, which means to call alongside and to exhort.

Let's practice our parakaleo—our encouragement—today.

## Scripture to Remember

*Therefore encourage one another and build up one another, just as you also are doing.*

1 Thessalonians 5:11

*Let no unwholesome word proceed from your mouth, but only such a word as is good for edification according to the need of the moment, so that it will give grace to those who hear.*

Ephesians 4:29

## Live It

* Reward your coworkers with a special treat, just because.
* Send encouraging texts.
* Leave notes in your kids' lunch bags.

# Keep Learning

Once we're out of school, a lot of us tend to think we know it all and close our minds to future education. We've wrapped our minds around what we believe. We've chosen our field or career and feel pretty stable.

But this is where we fail.

We wouldn't want to go to a doctor who hasn't updated his medical library or learned any of the new techniques in the past forty years, would we? What about taking our computer to a repair shop where the technician only knows DOS and hasn't updated to Windows? These extreme examples are pretty ridiculous, but they serve to illustrate that we can't get by on our own experience alone.

As long as we are living and breathing on this earth, we should continue learning. Most important, we should keep studying and learning about God and His Word. A stagnant Christian is useless. Break yourself of the mind-set that you can't teach an old dog new tricks.

> "Develop a passion for learning. If you do, you will never cease to grow."
>
> ANTHONY J. D'ANGELO

Never stop learning.

## Scripture to Remember

*Take My yoke upon you and learn from Me,*
*for I am gentle and humble in heart, and*
YOU WILL FIND REST FOR YOUR SOULS.

MATTHEW 11:29

*Teach me, O LORD, the way of Your statutes,*
*and I shall observe it to the end.*

PSALM 119:33

## Live It

* Make a commitment to read your Bible every day.
* Always seek to learn new things.
* Enroll in a class at a local or community college.
* Read a book on a subject you haven't studied before.

# Don't Procrastinate

Procrastination is a tough topic—especially when we're tempted to procrastinate on a job that isn't as pleasant as watching a movie or playing a game or surfing the net. In our world of incredible technology, we've come up with five billion ways to avoid the task at hand.

How can our work be honoring to the Lord if we put off what we should be doing? And if we should be doing our very best for Him, how can we make excuses for procrastinating?

> "Never put off till tomorrow what you can do today."
>
> THOMAS JEFFERSON

It's true that some people work better on deadlines, and schedules are a must, but that doesn't mean we should be waiting until the last minute to get projects done. Prioritizing and managing our time are the best ways to stop procrastination.

## Scripture to Remember

*"Therefore be on the alert, for you do*
*not know which day your Lord is coming."*

MATTHEW 24:42


*But all things must be done properly*
*and in an orderly manner.*

1 CORINTHIANS 14:40


## Live It

* Do the tasks you dislike the most first.
* Make a schedule and stick to it.
* Seek out an accountability partner.
* Avoid distractions.

# Put On the Armor of God

We often don't prepare for our days as Christians as meticulously as we fix our hair or follow our workout routine. But we are in a battle against the enemy, who seeks to destroy and keep us from sharing God's truth with others. We go about our business—work, school, church—and forget about the battle for souls being waged around us.

> "Folks, we are in a battle. Each and every day. Don't forget your armor."
>
> PASTOR GARRY HOGAN

Imagine what it would be like if we took care to fully arm ourselves every day and were ready to take our place in the Lord's army. Imagine the impact we could have and the souls we could win for Christ. It's an awesome task. You might be thinking that you aren't ready for it, but we all are—because our Commander has given us the tools we need. Truth, righteousness, faith, salvation, and the Holy Spirit. We should be wearing our armor just like we wear our clothes. Every day.

## Scripture to Remember

*Finally, be strong in the Lord and in the strength of His might. Put on the full armor of God, so that you will be able to stand firm against the schemes of the devil. For our struggle is not against flesh and blood, but against the rulers, against the powers, against the world forces of this darkness, against the spiritual forces of wickedness in the heavenly places. Therefore, take up the full armor of God, so that you will be able to resist in the evil day, and having done everything, to stand firm. Stand firm therefore, HAVING GIRDED YOUR LOINS WITH TRUTH, and HAVING PUT ON THE BREASTPLATE OF RIGHTEOUSNESS, and having shod YOUR FEET WITH THE PREPARATION OF THE GOSPEL OF PEACE; in addition to all, taking up the shield of faith with which you will be able to extinguish all the flaming arrows of the evil one. And take THE HELMET OF SALVATION, and the sword of the Spirit, which is the word of God.*

EPHESIANS 6:10–17

## Live It

* Begin your morning with scripture.
* Ask the Lord to guide you today in your battle.

# Follow Through

Do you finish what you start? Do you always do what you say you're going to do?

These two things are the foundation of following through. Years and years ago, a man's word was everything. Now? Not so much. In our busy lives, we're overbooked, over-engaged, and overstimulated. As a result, our word doesn't mean what it used to.

How do we change this? How do we show that Christians *are* different? We need to follow through. If we say we are going to do something, we need to do it. If we start something, we need to finish it, and it's all to be done for His glory.

> "Your reputation and integrity are everything. Follow through on what you say you're going to do. Your credibility can only be built over time, and it is built from the history of your words and actions."
>
> MARIA RAZUMICH-ZEC

So let's do the job right. Your word will become powerful to those around you.

## Scripture to Remember

*I have fought the good fight, I have*
*finished the course, I have kept the faith.*
2 TIMOTHY 4:7

*I can do all things through Him who strengthens me.*
PHILIPPIANS 4:13

## Live It

* Don't commit to anything unless you can
  follow through.
* Only start today what you know you will be
  able to finish.
* Ask friends to hold you accountable.

# Keep Trying

With 1,093 patents to his name, Thomas Edison is a great example of perseverance. A prolific inventor, he once said, "I have not failed. I've just found ten thousand ways that won't work."

Many of us would give up. And we often do. If only more of us had the attitude of Thomas Edison.

Remember that as believers, we are running a race; a race we will often want to quit. We will want to give up. We've fallen down too many times, hit too many hurdles, landed in too many mud puddles. We're tired—too many spiritual attacks have knocked us down, and life has gotten too hard. And yet, we know

> "Our greatest weakness lies in giving up. The most certain way to succeed is always to try just one more time."
>
> THOMAS EDISON

that we must keep our eyes on the finish line. That we need to keep going. That we can do all things through *Him*.

Today, take some time to refresh yourself. Spend an extra moment with God's Word and read Philippians 4:13. And always keep trying.

## Scripture to Remember

*And not only this, but we also exult in our tribulations, knowing that tribulation brings about perseverance.*

ROMANS 5:3

*In this you greatly rejoice, even though now for a little while, if necessary, you have been distressed by various trials, so that the proof of your faith, being more precious than gold which is perishable, even though tested by fire, may be found to result in praise and glory and honor at the revelation of Jesus Christ.*

1 PETER 1:6–7

## Live It

* When you're tempted to quit, try one more time.
* Encourage someone else to keep trying.
* Memorize Philippians 4:13.

# Create Boundaries

Boundaries aren't what they used to be. In fact, a lot of people don't know where they draw the line on certain subjects. The boundaries are blurred, and we've lost a clear sense of right and wrong.

Take this psychological study for example. A group of professionals took ten children to a field to play. In the middle of the field were tons of toys, playground equipment—everything small children love to play with. The adults left the children and went away. Observing from a place where their young charges couldn't see them, the adults studied the children's behavior. To their amazement, all the kids sat down and cried.

> "Boundaries are the guardians of life."
>
> UNKNOWN

In the next phase of the experiment, the adults came back and placed a small fence around the kids and the play area. Leaving for a second time, their findings were completely different. The children began to get up and play. They found comfort in the boundaries put in place for them.

Likewise, adults need to set boundaries for themselves, too. We need to guard our minds, our time, and our families. The only way to do this is to use the Bible as our guide and ultimate authority. God doesn't have blurry boundaries. We need to follow His lead.

## Scripture to Remember

*Be on the alert, stand firm in the faith,*
*act like men, be strong.*

1 CORINTHIANS 16:13

*It was for freedom that Christ set us free; therefore keep*
*standing firm and do not be subject again to a yoke of slavery.*

GALATIANS 5:1

## Live It

* Discuss setting boundaries with your family.
* Learn to say no.
* Stand firm when your boundaries are challenged.

# Seek His Presence

The busyness of our daily lives has overrun our time to really soak in God's presence. How many sunrises do you marvel at and enjoy? Sunsets? What about thunderstorms? Children's laughter?

Seeking the Lord's presence means to actively be seeking His will for our lives. Seeking His heart.

He gives us thousands of reminders of Himself every day. He's in the little things as well as the big things. Do you thank Him for it all? Do you take time to cherish each opportunity to be in His presence?

> "The Bible will keep you from sin, or sin will keep you from the Bible."
>
> DWIGHT L. MOODY

In seeking His presence, we are seeking to know Him better, and seeking to share Him more with the world. Let's seek His presence today and share it with everyone we meet.

## A Life That Matters: D.L. Moody

Dwight L. Moody wasn't a highly educated man. He didn't come from a family of means. But when Dwight found the Lord, the one-time shoe salesman sought His presence with everything in him. Working independently of church denominations and without any great theological, flowery words, Moody sought to bring souls to Christ. His preaching and heart-warming stories reached thousands upon thousands, and the Moody Church in Chicago and Moody Bible Institute are named in his honor.

## Scripture to Remember

*"But from there you will seek the LORD your God,*
*and you will find Him if you search for Him*
*with all your heart and all your soul."*

DEUTERONOMY 4:29

*Sow with a view to righteousness, reap in accordance with*
*kindness; break up your fallow ground, for it is time to seek the*
*LORD until He comes to rain righteousness on you.*

HOSEA 10:12

*"Ask, and it will be given to you; seek, and you will find;*
*knock, and it will be opened to you."*

MATTHEW 7:7

*Therefore if you have been raised up with Christ,*
*keep seeking the things above, where Christ is,*
*seated at the right hand of God.*

COLOSSIANS 3:1

## Live It

✳ Spend time with the Word each and every day.
✳ Remind yourself that God is omnipresent—
   He is always with you.
✳ Praise Him in the car on the way to work.
✳ Take thirty seconds to silently marvel at His
   creation.

# Pray without Ceasing

Would your relationship with your spouse grow if you didn't talk every day? What about your relationship with your kids? Do you ignore them and not speak to them? How about your close friends? If you didn't stay in touch with them, never returned phone calls, e-mails, or messages—do you think the relationship would survive?

The same is true of our relationship with our heavenly Father. He longs for us to get to know Him better. He wants to be involved in our everyday lives. He sees all, He knows all, and yet, He cares about every little detail. He is there to comfort us. To sustain us. To encourage us. To refresh us.

> "Prayer is simply a two-way conversation between you and God."
>
> BILLY GRAHAM

He's given us this life, and it matters so very much to Him. He wants to be involved. But He's not going to force His way in. Our job is to keep those lines of communication open. The Bible is clear about praying constantly. We are to pray without ceasing. That means, yes, you can talk to God anytime you want. About anything.

Let's get off the crazy merry-go-round of life and remember our Creator. Pray every chance you get. He's your best friend, just waiting on the other end of the line for *you*.

## Scripture to Remember

*Pray without ceasing.*

1 Thessalonians 5:17

*It was at this time that He went off to the mountain to pray,
and He spent the whole night in prayer to God.*

Luke 6:12

## Live It

* Begin the day by starting a conversation with God.
* Thank God for the source of your happiness.
* Share your burdens with Him when you are sad.
* Make a habit to build your relationship with the Lord.

# Cease Striving

We often make up our minds about something we want or want to do, and we think, "God must want that for me." And off we go. Then we wonder why it's never quite as satisfying as we thought it would be.

Along with being still and seeking God's will for our lives, we need to cease striving after things we haven't first laid at His feet. Forcing an issue when we haven't bathed it in prayer.

> "Stop pushing and pulling and forcing and striving for something that may not need to be. Our own desires, wills, and wants may not be what the Master has for us."
>
> UNKNOWN

In our stubbornness and eagerness to be in control, we often yank the reins away from God and basically say, "I've got it. I wanna do it my way."

But what if we were totally surrendered to Him? What if today you gave Him everything you had and said, "Lord, take me, use me, and mold me into what *You* want me to be." Wouldn't that be amazing? To allow the Master Potter to have total control in shaping you?

Sometimes in our quest to live lives that matter, we strive for the wrong things. This is your reminder to slow down and seek His will. His plans are *always* better than our own.

## Scripture to Remember

*Be anxious for nothing, but in everything*
*by prayer and supplication with thanksgiving*
*let your requests be made known to God.*

PHILIPPIANS 4:6

## Live It

* Give the longings of your heart to God.
* Align your goals with God's goals for your life.
* Stop. Take a breath. Wait for His guidance.

# Be Hospitable

When we think of hospitality, we often think of a grand hostess in a beautiful home. Lavish decor and a lot of good food. But hospitality can be so much more than that. It's meeting the needs of others. Being generous with our things. Listening more than we speak. Opening our hearts.

> "As for ourselves, yes, we must be meek, bear injustice, malice, rash judgment. We must turn the other cheek, give up our cloak, go a second mile."
>
> DOROTHY DAY

In our quest to live our lives in a way that's worthy of our Lord and Savior, we need to first and foremost share His love. That's what hospitality is all about. Opening your door to a neighbor who's locked out of the house. Taking cookies or brownies to your kid's coach just because. Fixing a friend's plumbing. Building a fence. Waving at your neighbors as you pass them on the street. Driving in a courteous manner on the interstate. Offering a hug to someone who's hurting. Sending a card. Opening your home to a Bible study or teen group.

We're all blessed with different gifts, and we can be hospitable in so many ways. So let's get out there and share God's love.

## Scripture to Remember

*Be hospitable to one another without complaint. As each one has received a special gift, employ it in serving one another as good stewards of the manifold grace of God.*

1 PETER 4:9–10

## Live It

* Open up your home for dinner to a needy family.
* Offer someone a ride to work or to the store.
* Offer your time to pray for the leaders in your church.
* Start a hospitality ministry at your church if there isn't one.
* Welcome newcomers in your neighborhood, office, or church with a handwritten card.

# Pray before Every Decision

Decisions, decisions, decisions. Everywhere we go, we need to make decisions. And often hindsight tells us that we've made the wrong one.

The best way to combat this problem is to pray before making a final judgment. No matter how big or small, we need to bring our concerns before God. Don't wait until you have nowhere else to go. As soon as the

> "I have been driven many times upon my knees by the overwhelming conviction that I had nowhere else to go. My own wisdom and that of all about me seemed insufficient for that day."
>
> ABRAHAM LINCOLN

need arises, take it to the Father in prayer. And if we're keeping those communication lines open, we should be praying without ceasing anyway.

Praying before a decision will also keep you from making rash judgments and impulse purchases that you'll regret later. If you pray about a decision, it could also keep you from saying something you shouldn't.

## Scripture to Remember

> *Be anxious for nothing, but in everything by prayer*
> *and supplication with thanksgiving let your requests*
> *be made known to God. And the peace of God,*
> *which surpasses all comprehension, will guard*
> *your hearts and your minds in Christ Jesus.*
>
> PHILIPPIANS 4:6–7

## Live It

* Commit to prayer before every decision.
* Ask a friend to hold you accountable.
* Seek the Father's guidance.
* Make a note to remind yourself: "Pray first. Answer second."

# Practice What You Preach

Too often Christians are labeled as hypocrites because of how they talk at work, how they act when they drive, how they do business, or how they treat people when they leave the church building. It's sad, but it is true.

The enemy loves this. He loves to showcase instances where Christians don't practice what they preach. But we can change that by living lives that matter, taking everything one day at a time, and working on our words and our actions.

Thought and prayer should come before our words. Are you thinking things through before you say them? Or would you rather have a holier-than-thou attitude and spout off whatever scripture comes to

> "I have a perfect horror of words that are not backed up by deeds."
> THEODORE ROOSEVELT

mind? Or mandate how others should clean up their lives when there's plenty to clean up in your own, just like the Bible tells us not to pick at a speck in a fellow Christian's eye when there's a log sticking out of our own eye?

To be examples of Christ on this journey, we need to be practicing what we preach. If we say something, we need to back it up with action.

## Scripture to Remember

*If we say that we have fellowship with Him and yet walk in the darkness, we lie and do not practice the truth.*

1 JOHN 1:6

## Live It

* Don't drive in an ungodly, ugly, or angry manner.
* Don't just be a Sunday Christian.
* Do share scripture with your family and coworkers.
* Do follow through on what you say.

# Love God, Love Others

The greatest commandments in the Bible are to love the Lord our God, and then to love others.

When we love the Lord with our heart, soul, mind, and strength, our passion for Him grows on a daily basis. We yearn to be in His presence. We long to hear His Word. We can't get enough of who He is.

That love and passion will bubble up and spill over like a beautiful fountain onto the people around you. When you truly love God, you can't help but love the people around you. Yes, even the obnoxious, annoying, and trying ones around you.

> "When you love you wish to do things for. You wish to sacrifice for. You wish to serve."
>
> ERNEST HEMINGWAY

God loves all of us the same. Despite our flaws. Despite our sin. Despite our shortcomings. Despite our annoying traits. Isn't that encouraging? To know the God of the universe cares about each one of us so very much? That He loves you and me, quirks and all?

That's an incredible portrait of love. We need to return that love to Him and praise Him for all He's done. And then we need to follow His commandments: Love the Lord, your God, and love your neighbor as yourself.

## Scripture to Remember

*Beloved, if God so loved us, we also ought to love one another.*
1 JOHN 4:11

*You shall love the LORD your God with all your heart and with all your soul and with all your might.*
DEUTERONOMY 6:5

*And He said to him, "'YOU SHALL LOVE THE LORD YOUR GOD WITH ALL YOUR HEART, AND WITH ALL YOUR SOUL, AND WITH ALL YOUR MIND.' This is the great and foremost commandment. The second is like it, 'YOU SHALL LOVE YOUR NEIGHBOR AS YOURSELF.'"*
MATTHEW 22:37–39

## Live It

* Wake up and sing, "I Love You, Lord."
* Praise Him on the way to work.
* Memorize Matthew 22:37–39 and 1 John 4:11.
* Offer to buy your least favorite person lunch.

# Listen

Being a good friend, a good spouse, a good employee, and a good employer are all key aspects of living a life that matters. To be great—even good—at any of those listed above, you've got to be a good listener. Not the first one to give advice or give an opinion. The first one to L-I-S-T-E-N.

Listening is different than hearing. James said that we must be doers of the Word and not just hearers. Listening is that part in between. We *hear* all kinds of stuff. But a lot of it really is in one ear and out the other. Listening is an act of participation on our part. To listen, you must be tuned in and absorb the information that's being passed to you.

> "The reason why we have two ears and only one mouth is that we may listen the more and talk the less."
>
> ZENO OF CITIUM

It can make or break your Christian walk, your marriage, your job, and your relationships with your kids. You've got to listen to wise counsel, your boss's recommendations, your coworkers' ideas, your family members' hurts.

Take the time to really listen to what people are saying around you. Watch their body language, ask questions, and find out if they are hiding their hurts underneath their outer facade.

## Scripture to Remember

*A time to be silent and a time to speak.*
ECCLESIASTES 3:7


*"Why do you call Me, 'Lord, Lord,'*
*and do not do what I say?"*
LUKE 6:46


*Listen to counsel and accept discipline,*
*that you may be wise the rest of your days.*
PROVERBS 19:20


*It is better to listen to the rebuke of a wise*
*man than for one to listen to the song of fools.*
ECCLESIASTES 7:5

## Live It

* Take turns talking about everyone's day around the dinner table.
* Use constructive criticism to your advantage.
* Don't be the first one to offer advice.
* Seek out wise counsel, and be humble as you listen.

# Be Willing to Change and Grow

Stagnancy in the Christian life is unacceptable. In fact, scripture says that He would rather us be hot or cold because if we're lukewarm, He'd like to spew us out of His mouth. Most people would choose *not* to be spewed anywhere. It's a lot like eating a rotten apple or moldy bread. At first taste, you'd spit it right out.

Typically, the older we get, the more set in our ways we become. We say things like, "Well that's the way it's always been done." And yet, Jesus challenges us to continue to grow. Continue to study His Word. Continue to change as He molds us.

> "Change is the end result of all true learning."
>
> LEO BUSCAGLIA

Our world is constantly changing, and to be a light for it, we need to change as well. He is the Potter, and we are the clay. Let's not get all dried out and unworkable. Let's be willing to change.

## Scripture to Remember

> *"So because you are lukewarm, and neither*
> *hot nor cold, I will spit you out of My mouth."*
> REVELATION 3:16

> *"And you will know the truth,*
> *and the truth will make you free."*
> JOHN 8:32

## Live It

* Try something new today.
* Identify stagnant areas of your life, and improve them for the better.
* Listen to ideas from others.

# Choose Righteousness

Are you willing to choose the narrow path no matter the cost? Choosing righteousness isn't always going to be the popular choice. It's not going to be the easy choice. But it is the *only* choice we should make.

What if Jesus were in front of you today and said, "Come, follow Me." Would you be like the rich man? Jesus told him to go sell everything he owned and follow Him. But the rich man couldn't do it. Or would you be like one of the others who requested to bid their families good-bye first? Or the man who asked to go bury his father? What choice would you make?

> "If I must choose between righteousness and peace, I choose righteousness."
> THEODORE ROOSEVELT

Our Lord is waiting for us to make the simple choice to follow Him no matter what. No ifs, ands, or buts about it.

To make the commitment to choose righteousness, we must be willing to choose Him over *anything* and *everything* else.

# A Life That Matters: John and Betty Stam

John and Betty Stam were missionaries with the China Inland Mission during the Chinese Civil War. In 1934, communist soldiers came for them and their three-month-old daughter, Helen. After the communists demanded all the Stams' money, John and Betty were eventually taken to the local prison and then marched to their executions at Miaosheo. A letter from John to the mission authorities was found among Helen's clothes after their deaths. At the end of the letter he wrote, "Philippians 1:20: May Christ be glorified whether by life or death." The story of the Stams' deaths for Christ gained publicity around the world and inspired many to become missionaries.

## Scripture to Remember

*So you will walk in the way of good men*
*and keep to the paths of the righteous.*

PROVERBS 2:20

*"I put on righteousness, and it clothed me."*

JOB 29:14

*I will rejoice greatly in the LORD, my soul will exult*
*in my God; for He has clothed me with garments*
*of salvation, He has wrapped me with a robe of*
*righteousness, as a bridegroom decks himself with a*
*garland, and as a bride adorns herself with her jewels.*

ISAIAH 61:10

## Live It

* Do something kind for another person.
* Pray for others.
* Make a sacrifice for someone else today.
* Pick one characteristic of Jesus and mimic it today.
* Don't give in to lusts or temptations.

# Look in the Mirror

We are fearfully and wonderfully made. Our wondrous Creator knows us inside and out. He knows our most intimate thoughts. He understands our deepest hurts. He shares our biggest dreams.

But we were created in the image of God—to *glorify* God. That means each and every day we need to be looking in the mirror, examining our reflection. Are we shining His light? Are we reflecting Christ everywhere we go?

If we are truly reflecting Christ, then just like the Lewis quote beside, we should be seeing everything through Him. The hurting people around us. The needy around us. The lost. The broken.

> "I believe in Christianity as I believe that the sun has risen: not only because I see it, but because by it I see everything else."
>
> C.S. Lewis

Not only do we need to wear our reflection of Christ, but we need to see through it. Our salvation is the greatest gift ever, and we need to see others as Christ did and does. He didn't see us as damaged beyond repair. No. He saw beautiful children of God who needed salvation. He came to die for each and every one of us. He sacrificed Himself so that we might all have the opportunity to live for eternity with Him.

So take a look in the mirror. Are you mirroring Christ? And are you seeing through His eyes?

Look around you today and love as Jesus loves.

## Scripture to Remember

*But we all, with unveiled face, beholding as in a mirror the glory of the Lord, are being transformed into the same image from glory to glory, just as from the Lord, the Spirit.*

2 CORINTHIANS 3:18

## Live It

* Think about what Jesus would do when you face a tough decision.
* Ask yourself often, "Am I reflecting Christ?"

# Be Still

Our fast-paced, high-tech society keeps us busy. Often too busy to spend time with God's Word. There's always a ball game to watch, extra time at the office, meals to cook, or kids to shuttle from one practice to another. Is this you? When was the last time you were still and focused on the Lord?

> "Every day has exactly 1,440 minutes; can't you find even ten of them to be with your heavenly Father? Doesn't God deserve the best minutes of your day?"
>
> BILLY GRAHAM

Jesus was the perfect example for us. When the crowds got too big and He needed time alone to pray and meditate, He sent them away. He loved serving and teaching, but He also took time to be still. Time to rejuvenate and reflect on God's Word.

Our first priority shouldn't be paying the bills or getting to that all-important meeting. It should be making that appointment with our heavenly Father. Those precious moments of being still and knowing that He is God will make a huge difference in every minute of your day.

## Scripture to Remember

*And He got up and rebuked the wind and said to the sea, "Hush, be still." And the wind died down and it became perfectly calm.*

MARK 4:39

*He says, "Be still, and know that I am God."*

PSALM 46:10 NIV

*Rest in the LORD and wait patiently for Him.*

PSALM 37:7

## Live It

* Give God the first and last few minutes of every day.
* Take devotional breaks at work.
* Pray as you're driving.

# Do Good Deeds

When you think of doing good deeds, do you think of what you'll get in return? We're all pretty willing to do things that will get us recognized, but what about anonymous deeds? How often is the janitor thanked in the church bulletin? Or the woman at church who visits all the shut-ins? How about the person who makes coffee for everyone on Sunday mornings? Sometimes we know who does these jobs, and sometimes we don't. But they are all things that need to be done.

> "There are many of us that are willing to do great things for the Lord, but few of us are willing to do little things."
> DWIGHT L. MOODY

All the little jobs matter, whether they are recognized or not. And the Bible is clear that others will know we are His believers, children of God, by our good works.

So why not offer to help clean up after an office party or set up chairs for your children's play? You could fix meals for someone who's laid up or just bring a dessert to lift someone's spirits. All the little things matter as well. Opening doors, offering a helping hand, and giving a note of encouragement all show the love of Christ. Take some time this week to do some good works for Him.

## Scripture to Remember

*For we are His workmanship, created in*
*Christ Jesus for good works, which God prepared*
*beforehand so that we would walk in them.*

EPHESIANS 2:10

*"Let your light shine before men in such*
*a way that they may see your good works,*
*and glorify your Father who is in heaven."*

MATTHEW 5:16

## Live It

* Open the door for at least one person today.
* Fix a surprise meal or brownies for a neighbor.
* Mow an elderly neighbor's lawn.

# Be a Light

In this sin-filled world, we are called to be a light in the darkness. Using our individual talents and gifts, we can shine that light to others.

Whether you shovel snow or clean toilets for a living, God can use you right where you are to be His light. Some people can share their musical ability to shine His light. Some people can take care to clean public restrooms, and that can shine His light. Some people speak in front of thousands and shine His light. Some people share stories on a more personal level and shine His light.

> "We are told to let our light shine, and if it does, we won't need to tell anybody it does. Lighthouses don't fire cannons to call attention to their shining—they just shine."
>
> DWIGHT L. MOODY

No matter the job, no matter how large or small, God wants us to be light for Him. He longs for other people to see *Him* in us and to ask, "Hey, what's different about you?"

You're never too young or too old to be a light for Christ. Don't hide your light under a bushel. Let it shine. Don't let Satan blow it out. Let it shine till Jesus comes.

## A Life That Matters: C.S. Lewis

Clive Staples Lewis was an author who still impacts the world with his stories. A close friend of J.R.R. Tolkien and a leading figure in Oxford University's English department, Lewis gained wide acclaim with his radio broadcasts on the subject of Christianity during the war. His most popular fictional works, *The Chronicles of Narnia*, have been read by millions around the world, and the stories' immense popularity have seen them turned into major motion pictures. Through his love of story, Lewis was able to shine the light of Christ around the globe. Other books by Lewis, such as *The Screwtape Letters* and *Mere Christianity*, also continue to change people's lives through the written word.

## Scripture to Remember

> *"You are the light of the world."*
> MATTHEW 5:14

> *"Let your light shine before men in such
> a way that they may see your good works,
> and glorify your Father who is in heaven."*
> MATTHEW 5:16

> *Therefore do not be partakers with them; for you were
> formerly darkness, but now you are Light in the Lord;
> walk as children of Light (for the fruit of the Light
> consists in all goodness and righteousness and truth).*
> EPHESIANS 5:7–9

## Live It

* Smile at others today.
* Extend an encouraging word to everyone around you.
* Don't hide the fact that you are a believer.
* Let it shine.

# Give

In this day and age of "Show me the money!", giving is declining. Churches struggle. Ministries struggle. Charities struggle. People are keeping more of their wealth for themselves.

But giving isn't just about financial needs. We've also become selfish in our giving of time, work, service, and even love. We horde all these things for ourselves and those we hold most dear.

> "Show me your hands. Do they have scars from giving? Show me your feet. Are they wounded in service? Show me your heart. Have you left a place for divine love?"
>
> FULTON J. SHEEN

We can change that. As believers, we should be as generous as we can. We should be feeding the hungry, comforting the hurting, giving shelter to the orphans and homeless. It's all about giving. Do you have a mind-set for giving? Are you willing to give?

In Matthew chapter five, Jesus is preaching the Sermon on the Mount. When we are wronged, He instructs us to give the other cheek, give more than just the shirt—give our coat as well. So how much *more* should we give when we give cheerfully?

Giving should start in our heart. Remember, we're not taking any of our "stuff" with us. We can give monetarily. We can give food. We can give clothing. We can give time. We can give love, showing God's love through each and every gift.

## Scripture to Remember

*"In everything I showed you that by working hard*
*in this manner you must help the weak and remember*
*the words of the Lord Jesus, that He Himself said,*
*'It is more blessed to give than to receive.'"*
ACTS 20:35

*Each one must do just as he has purposed in his heart, not*
*grudgingly or under compulsion, for God loves a cheerful giver.*
2 CORINTHIANS 9:7

## Live It

* ✳ Give cheerfully today and every day.
* ✳ Give of your time, money, services, and talent.

# Be Faithful

*Faithful.* The word encompasses so much. Thoroughness in the performance of duty. Commitment to one's promises. Loyalty and steadfast allegiance.

All these elements of faithfulness are hard to live up to. And as sinful human beings, almost impossible! But Jesus is the perfect example. He lived out faithfulness, and the challenge is set before us to mirror Him.

> "As I look back over fifty years of ministry I recall innumerable tests, trials and times of crushing pain. But through it all, the Lord has proven faithful, loving, and totally true to all His promises."
>
> DAVID WILKERSON

First, we should start off by being faithful in the small things: honoring our word, following through, and being an honest and loyal friend. And then by being faithful in the big things: honoring our spouse and not allowing temptation of any kind a foothold in our lives. A faithful follower will follow the steps of the Master in front of Him.

## Scripture to Remember

*A faithful man will abound with blessings.*
PROVERBS 28:20

*Faithful is He who calls you,*
*and He also will bring it to pass.*
1 THESSALONIANS 5:24

*But the Lord is faithful, and He will*
*strengthen and protect you from the evil one.*
2 THESSALONIANS 3:3

## Live It

* Make a list of areas in your life where you
  could be more faithful.
* Let your yes be yes and your no be no.
* Guard your mind.
* Avoid triggers that could lead to unfaithfulness.

# Don't Worry

Worry is that ever-present voice in the back of our minds. The "what-if" question that enslaves our days. Many medical studies have focused on worry and how it affects our bodies physically. It causes heart disease, heart attacks, strokes, muscles spasms, high blood pressure, ulcers, headaches, migraines—the list could go on and on.

But what is at the root of worry? Fear. Plain and simple, ugly, old fear.

In the parable of the sower, Jesus illustrates that His Word is seed and the different types of ground are like different types of people—recipients—of His Word. The analogy of seeds falling among thorns being like the choking "worry of the world" speaks volumes about the negative impact of worry in our lives. We need to defeat worry because it is a sin and hinders us from the blessings of the Lord.

> "Worry never robs tomorrow of its sorrow, it only saps today of its joy."
> LEO BUSCAGLIA

## A Life That Matters: George Müller

The greatest undertaking of George Müller was the orphanages in Bristol, England. He started with only two shillings (fifty cents), and without worry—or even letting anyone know the needs—fed and sheltered thousands of orphans. Many times, there was no food for the coming meal, but Mr. Mü ller didn't worry. He prayed to God and left his needs up to Him. In time, over $7,000,000 was sent to him for the construction and maintenance of new orphanages. Food would often arrive on the doorstep just in time to feed everyone. What an awesome example of a life without worry.

## Scripture to Remember

*"And the one on whom seed was sown among the thorns, this is the man who hears the word, and the worry of the world and the deceitfulness of wealth choke the word, and it becomes unfruitful."*

MATTHEW 13:22

*"Do not worry then, saying, 'What will we eat?' or 'What will we drink?' or 'What will we wear for clothing?'"*

MATTHEW 6:31

*"And which of you by worrying can add a single hour to his life's span?"*

LUKE 12:25

*"So do not worry about tomorrow; for tomorrow will care for itself. Each day has enough trouble of its own."*

MATTHEW 6:34

## Live It

✳ When you are tempted to give in to worry, pray.

✳ Always look on the bright side.

✳ Give God control.

# Live Your Life–
## It's a Life That Matters

Our God is so amazing. He created us in His image. He breathed life into us. He gave us the gift of free will. And then we messed up. Sin corrupted God's perfect creation. Yet He still loves us. So much so that He sent His only Son as a sacrifice on our behalf—so that we might have eternity with Him.

We stumble, we fall, we give in to temptation time and again. But He's always there, waiting for us with open arms. That's why it's so important as believers to keep going, to confess our sin and not wallow in the self-pity and doubt that usually accompanies our guilt.

> "When I stand before God at the end of my life, I would hope that I would not have a single bit of talent left, and could say, 'I used everything You gave me.'"
>
> ERMA BOMBECK

God has given each of us a life that matters. He wants us to use it for Him.

Get out there. Run your race. Live life abundantly. Throw off those encumbrances. Cast off that sin. Because you matter to God. Each and every moment of every single day.

## Scripture to Remember

*Therefore, since we have so great a cloud of witnesses
surrounding us, let us also lay aside every encumbrance and
the sin which so easily entangles us, and let us run with
endurance the race that is set before us, fixing our eyes on Jesus,
the author and perfecter of faith, who for the joy set before
Him endured the cross, despising the shame, and has sat down
at the right hand of the throne of God. For consider Him who
has endured such hostility by sinners against Himself, so that
you will not grow weary and lose heart.*

HEBREWS 12:1–3

## Live It

* Begin each day confessing your sin to God.
* Give Him the glory during even the smallest tasks.
* Encourage someone else to keep moving forward.
* Don't look back.

# Scripture Index